UFOS OVER
SOUTH CAROLINA

Sherman Carmichael

4880 Lower Valley Road • Atglen, PA 19310

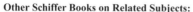
For our complete selection of fine books on this and related subjects, please visit our website at: www.schifferbooks.com. You may also write for a free catalog.

This book may be purchased from the publisher. Please try your bookstore first.

We are always looking for people to write books on new and related subjects. If you have an idea for a book, please contact us at proposals@schifferbooks.com.

Schiffer Publishing's titles are available at special discounts for bulk purchases for sales promotions or premiums. Special editions, including personalized covers, corporate imprints, and excerpts can be created in large quantities for special needs. For more information, contact the publisher.

CONTENTS

PREFACE

The subject of UFOs has been a controversial one from the time people started discussing them. Some people believe in them, some don't. Whether UFOs exist or not is still speculation—or is it?

The stories in this book have been taken from the files of many UFO organizations and individuals. The original information was written in report format, but for the purpose of this book it has been transformed into story format. The information in these stories is exactly what came from the reports—nothing has been added or taken away. There are several stories where I interviewed the witnesses; their stories are exactly what were said in the interview. Remember: when someone sees something that they can't explain or think it's an alien space craft, through excitement or fear facts become distorted. These people believe what they saw. I have no reason to believe that they are not telling the truth. These stories are recorded exactly according to what they saw. As the author, it's not my place to give an opinion on these reports. I am just presenting the facts as I have gathered them.

Three things form the basis of all research: Freedom of thought; The gift of observation; and Sense of context.

– Author Eric Von Daniken

THE UFO MYSTERY

What is the driving force that continues to make man search the heavens for life? Curiosity…the little voice inside of us that never stops asking questions. Day after day, night after night, year after year, we keep watching the heavenly luminaries in search of the answers. Will we ever find the answers we're looking for? For those looking for life on other planets, maybe they're looking in the wrong direction. Maybe that life has come to visit us.

On July 20, 1969, at 20:17:39, *Apollo 11* landed on the lunar surface with three astronauts on board: Commander Neil Armstrong, Command Module pilot Michael Collins, and Lunar Module pilot Buzz Aldrin. At 10:56 EDT, Commander Neil Armstrong was the first human to step on the moon. Nineteen minutes later Buzz Aldrin was the second human to step on the moon. We landed on another world in 1969, so maybe beings from another world are landing on ours today.

UFOs have been recorded since ancient times. Ancient paintings and carvings depict what appears to be some type of being in a spacesuit. Ancient flying machines have been painted and carved on rocks as far back as recorded history. The first recorded UFO sighting was 332 B.C.

Let's fast forward to the future, say to 1909, and the great airship scare. Let's zip on up to World War I, 1917, with the scare ships. Let's travel a few more years into the future to 1933-34, the ghost flyers. Let's go to World War II and the Foo Fighters. In 1945, we had the galloping ghosts. In 1946, we had the ghost rockets. Over the years, there have been quite a few different names for the Unidentified Flying Objects, but one thing is certain — they have been witnessed on every part of the globe.

On June 24, 1947, Kenneth Arnold was flying over the Cascade Mountains in Washington State when he noticed nine silver objects flying near Mt. Rainer. Arnold reported that the objects moved like saucers skipping across water. The term "flying saucer" was born — or was it? On a cold January day in 1878, a Texas farmer described an object flying over him as about the size of a saucer.

There have been many theories about UFOs and what they are and where they come from. Of course, the government says they don't exist. The government is good at covering things up when they can't explain it or don't want American citizens to know about it. Would the government admit they exist if they could exploit it and make money for themselves? Some government explanations are temperature inversions, cold weather inversions, air sandwiches caused by low-lying cold air that traps radar signals, mirages, thousand-mile-an-hour weather balloons, off-course airplanes, the planet Venus, or mass hallucinations. However, there is a real good possible explanation for a few UFOs. With an increasing number of humans happily over-indulging in their favorite spirits (not ghosts), do they manage to manifest things in their minds like UFOs, pink elephants, and an assortment of purple polka-dotted animals? Does the human mind have enough power to manifest thought forms?

Unidentified Flying Object

On many UFO reports much of the information is left out, inaccurate, misunderstood, or simply made up. Many UFO reports are made by unidentified witnesses who cannot be verified. This tends to lead the investigator to believe that it was not a creditable UFO sighting.

Many UFO sightings are nothing more than misidentified objects or less-than-welcome invaders — meteorites. However, many UFO sightings have been reported where the UFO appears to be under some kind of intelligent control.

UFOs have been a difficult problem for the human race to believe, even though they go as far back as recorded history. Pictures of flying objects and beings in spacesuits were painted on cave walls before people could write.

Why has it been so difficult for humans to deal with the UFO phenomena? The human race would like to believe that we're the only intelligent, *if not the only*, living beings in existence today. We don't want to believe that we're just a little speck in the endless heavens or that there are beings out there that are far superior to us. To find that we are not alone and may still be in a primitive state compared to other beings from somewhere out there would be a devastating blow to the ego of the human race, so most just close their eyes and simply refuse to believe UFOs and aliens exist.

The media has only been too happy to ridicule those who claim to have seen a UFO and those who take UFOs seriously. Heaven forbid if someone reports alien contact or an alien abduction! Maybe this is why serious witnesses are afraid to come forward.

UFO witnesses and their families have been threatened by all branches of the government. For instance, those mysterious men in black who make an occasional appearance — long enough to threaten the witness and their family — and then disappear. Of course, the government disavows any knowledge that these men exist.

After you make a UFO report, you're left in a state of aloneness, with everyone thinking you've gone bananas. Even the people you thought were your friends start looking at you like you're sitting there on a rock, staring at the moon.

Many people believe that the word UFO means a spacecraft operated by aliens or some form of life other than humans. Many people believe these visitors from somewhere else are USO (unidentified submerged objects) and that they're coming from under the sea.

Many investigators are now referring to the UFO as an UAP (unidentified aerial phenomenon) because most sightings can be explained. Many of the sightings are simply misidentified by the witness.

Some ancient astronaut theorist would like you to believe that the Bible is the first written document of an encounter where a human left with an alien.

The Second Book of Kings, chapter 2 verse 11
"Then it happened, as they continued on and talked that suddenly a chariot of fire appeared with horses of fire, and separated the two of them; and Elijah went up by a whirlwind into heaven."

Exodus, chapter 19 verse 18
"Now Mount Sinai was completely in smoke because the Lord descended upon it in a fire. Its smoke ascended like the smoke of a furnace and the whole mountain quaked."

Ezekiel, chapter 1 verse 4
Then I looked and behold a whirlwind was coming out of the north, a great cloud with raging fire engulfing itself; and the brightness was all around it and radiating out of its midst like the color of amber, out of the midst of the fire.

Also from within it come the likeness of four living creatures, and this was their appearance; they had the likeness of man.

Each one had four faces, and each one had four wings.

Their legs were straight, and the soles of their feet were like the soles of calves' feet. They sparkled like the color of burnished bronze.
The book of Ezekiel has many verses with this type of description.

Some people are afraid of what they don't understand while others are trying to find the truth no matter how elusive it may be. They want to know who they are. Where do they come from? What are they doing here and how did they get here?

UFO Classifications

Many people report different encounters with UFOs. Dr. J. Allen Hynek of Project Blue Book has given the following classifications to UFO encounters: Encounter of the first kind is spotting a UFO; encounter of the second kind is having some kind of associated physical effects; encounter of the third kind involves seeing beings with the UFO, and encounter of the fourth kind involves having humans abducted.

Based on the aforementioned classifications, on December 10, 1986, a seventeen-year-old Abbeville man had a close encounter of the first kind and a close encounter of the second kind. A CE1 is an observation of a UFO within 150 yards while a CE2 leaves landing traces or injuries to the witness. (This encounter also results in loss of memory.)

The witness was alone at the time of this encounter, which occurred at approximately 12:30 a.m. He heard a whirring/whining sound outside the house. He went outside to investigate the sound and noticed amber lights reflecting off the trees around the house. The UFO had four sets of amber lights; each set contained three rotating lights. The lights were so bright that the house and surrounding area were bathed in amber light.

He looked up and saw a shiny silver saucer/disc-shaped craft about ten feet above him. The craft was about thirty-five feet across and ten feet high. His house is on stilts, putting him about eight feet above the ground. The craft slowly moved from above the house and then descended to about eye level with the witness. The UFO hovered there for a few seconds and then returned to its original position over the house. After the UFO hovered there for several minutes, it moved about twenty feet away from the house.

UFO TERMS

APRO: Aerial Phenomenon Research Organization

Bolide: Exploding meteorite

CAP: Civil Air Patrol

CAUS: Citizens Against UFO Secrecy

CIA: Central Intelligence Agency

CR: Crash retrieval

CUFOS: Center for UFO Studies

ET: Extra-terrestrial

FOIA: Freedom of Information Act

FBI: Federal Bureau of Investigation

MARCEN: Mutual Anomaly Research Center and Evaluation Network

MIB: Men in black

Moon Suits: The kind of suit worn by astronauts

MOPP: Gear-chemical suits

MUFON: Mutual UFO Network

NASA: National Aeronautics and Space Administration

NIA: National Intelligence Agency

NIC: National Investigations Committee

NICAP: National Investigations Committee on Aerial Phenomena

NORAD: North American Air Defense Command

NTE: Non-terrestrial Entities

OD: Orbital debris

OSS: Office of Strategic Services

SETI: Search for Extra Terrestrial Intelligence

UAV: Unmanned aerial vehicle

UFO: Unidentified flying object

USAF: United States Air Force

USO: Unified submerged object

The UFO had a dome on top with a round opaque/transparent window. All the witness could make out from the window was that there was a low intensity light inside. The craft moved about two hundred yards away from the house, hovered there for several seconds, and then flew off at a forty-five degree angle toward the southeast and out of sight. The witness felt so terrified that he could not move. He reported that he had a gap in his memory from that night. He believes the encounter lasted for about five minutes.

The witness bumped into a friend that he hadn't seen in several years. His friend asked him whatever happened to the UFO. His friend said the witness had called him while the UFO was there, but the witness didn't remember being on the phone or even telling anyone about the UFO. The witness feels like something else happened that night, but can't remember what. The witness went on to graduate from college. He is a Vietnam veteran and spent three years on a United States Navy destroyer. He spent many hours as a lookout while at sea. He was trained to spot and identify missiles and all types of aircraft, both foreign and American. He has never observed or seen pictures of anything that matches what he saw in 1968.

The Government Still Monitors UFO Reports

The official position of the United States government is that it doesn't investigate UFOs any longer. The official response from the United States Air Force is that UFOs don't exist. The Air Force officially ended their Project Blue Book research program on December 17, 1969. There are still reports of military planes or helicopters being seen in the area of a UFO sighting or shortly after the sighting.

Many UFO witnesses have reported seeing military planes arriving during or shortly after a UFO was seen. Some witnesses have reported being visited by strange individuals, commonly known in UFO circles as "Men in Black." These men in black would urge the UFO witness not to follow up on the report and just forget what they had seen. Are these men in black government officials trying to cover up something?

Many people who witness UFOs prefer to remain anonymous for fear of public ridicule. They are afraid that people may think they're off their rocker or walking around talking to a light bulb.

SHAW AIR FORCE BASE

Shaw Air Force Base is a United States Air Force facility located near Sumter, South Carolina. Construction on the base began in 1941. Shaw Field was activated on August 30, 1941, and placed under the jurisdiction of the Army Air Corps Southeast Air Corps Training Center. Shaw Field was named in honor of World War I pilot, 1st Lt. Ervin David Shaw, a Sumter native. Shaw was one of the pioneer Americans to fly combat missions in World War I. On July 9, 1918, Shaw was returning from a reconnaissance mission over enemy territory when he was attacked by three enemy aircraft. Shaw managed to shoot down one of the enemy aircraft before being killed.

After World War II, the 20th Fighter Bomber squadron established their headquarters at Shaw Field. The name was later changed to Shaw Air Force Base. Shaw is one of the biggest military bases operated by the United States. The following UFO sightings have been reported near Shaw Air Force Base.

October 1, 1952, at 6:57 p.m.: 1st Lt. T.J. Pointer, a pilot of an RF-80 reconnaissance jet, was flying near Shaw Air Force Base when he spotted a single bright white light. The light flew straight, then vertical, and then it hovered before making an abrupt turn and disappearing. This happened during a twenty-three-minute attempt by the RF-80 reconnaissance jet to intercept the light. The pilot reported that the craft maneuvered like it was under some sort of intelligent control.

1984, at 11 a.m. (only date given): A serviceman stationed at Shaw Air Force Base was outside the barracks when he spotted a shiny disc-shaped object in the vicinity of an F4 fighter jet leaving the base. The disc-shaped object was about one-half the size of the jet. The object made a turn on its vertical axis and began to disappear from sight. The object then disappeared. The object was flying east towards Sumter, South Carolina. There was no pursuit by the disc-shaped object or the jet.

May 25th, at 7:46 p.m.: A witness was driving near the back of Shaw Air force Base when they spotted a cigar-shaped object slowly moving silently just above the treetops. At first the witness thought it was a blimp. They stopped the car and got out for a better look. The object was flying in the path of planes taking off and landing at Shaw Air Force Base. It slowly moved on out of sight.

"The nations of the world will have to unite for the next war will be an interplanetary war. The nations of Earth must someday make a common front against attack by people from other planets." ~ General Douglas MacArthur, 1955, *New York Times*

"Our Sun is one of a hundred billion stars in our galaxy. Our galaxy is one of billions of galaxies populating the universe. It would be the height of presumption to think that we are the only living thing in that enormous immensity." ~ Wernher Von Braun.

"I can assure you the flying saucers, given that they exist, are not constructed by any power on Earth." ~ President Harry Truman

"At no time, when the astronauts were in space were we alone: there was a constant surveillance by UFO's." ~ NASA astronaut Scott Carpenter

Some researchers postulate that intelligent extraterrestrial beings have visited the Earth in antiquity or prehistory and made contact with humans. These ancient space travelers are called ancient astronauts. Many believe that these ancient visitors left their signs here with the ancient buildings and technology. Are we still being visited?

First UFO Sighting in America

The first UFO sighting documented in America is believed to be in Massachusetts.

John Winthrop (1588-1649) has the distinction of being the first elected Governor of the Massachusetts Bay Colony. Winthrop was an English Puritan who, like many others, sought religious freedom in the New World. Winthrop arrived in Massachusetts in 1629. By the time he arrived, an English colony had already been established. The smallpox virus brought to the New World by the new settlers had wiped out many of the indigenous people. When Winthrop was informed of this, he looked at it as God's way of cleansing the land for the God-fearing Christians from England.

Perhaps John Winthrop's greatest legacy of all was his chronicles. Winthrop wrote down all the events that he had witnessed and the stories he had heard in a giant tome called *The History of New England From 1630 to 1649*. There was one entry that stands out from the rest. The date was 1638 or 1639 (depending on what resource you use) when Winthrop documented the first UFO sighting in America. Winthrop wrote:

> James Everell and two others saw a great light in the night at Muddy River. When it was still, it flamed up and was about three yard square; when it ran, it ran as swift as an arrow towards Charlton and so far about two or three hours. They come down in their lighter about a mile and when it was over they found themselves carried quite back against the tide to the place they came from.

Did the UFO push the witnesses and their boat back out into the water against the tide?

MURRELLS INLET

The land that is now Murrells Inlet has a record of settlements that go back thousands of years before written history. Its early history is evident by the shell mounds and archeological findings. The pages of Murrells Inlet's history are graced with the footprints of American Indian tribes, sixteenth century Spanish explorers, and English colonists in the seventeenth century.

Murrells Inlet is one of the oldest coastal communities in South Carolina. It was settled in 1731 by English colonist John Murrall.

In the 1730s, the first planters arrived and began building settlements. By 1850, Murrells Inlet rice plantations were producing forty-seven million pounds of rice. In 1863, the Civil War came to Murrells Inlet, where Naval forces blockaded South Carolina ports. Damage to the rice fields, caused by hurricanes, including one often referred to as the Great Storm of 1893, ultimately ended the production of rice.

Murrells Inlet is legendary as the place where hush puppies (fried cornbread) were invented. It's also where Blackbeard and other notorious pirates are believed to have stashed their ill-gotten treasure. Today, Murrells Inlet is the seafood capital of South Carolina and a major tourist town.

There are several theories as to the reason so many UFOs are seen around Murrells Inlet. One is that people are outside almost twenty-four hours a day, year-round. Another theory is that the UFOs are coming up out of the ocean. There are those UFO hunters that believe that UFO bases are located on the ocean floor.

July 30, 1978, at 11:50 p.m.: The witness was with his grandfather, who was a big believer in UFOs. The grandfather was a World War II veteran, a radar specialist, and at one time was a B24 bomber pilot. He was familiar with the sky, the stars, weather, and air traffic. The witness stated that the UFO flew above their heads. The witness's description was that the object looked like a large ribbon tied together. Lights of every color reflected down on them. The grandfather told the witness not to be afraid, that the UFO was not a manned vehicle. They stood and watched as it went out over the ocean. The sighting lasted about two minutes.

May 8, 2000: Some vacationers were spending the week at Murrells Inlet, South Carolina. The second night they noticed orange orbs or lights about two miles out over the ocean. It was high enough to be seen above the houses in front of the witnesses. The lights were an orange color and about the size of a streetlight. The lights would just appear out of nowhere. They were too high to be the lights from a boat. The lights would slowly dim and fade out. A few minutes later, they would appear again and slowly dim and fade out. One time, two lights appeared and slowly faded out. The lights would appear and then slowly fade out one after the other. This happened several nights in a row at the same location. The light show lasted about two hours. There were no clouds in the sky.

October 22, 2003: A couple was on their pontoon boat about an eighth-of-a-mile past the jetties in Murrells Inlet, South Carolina, fishing. The sky was clear and sunny. They noticed a bright flash of light, as if the sun had reflected off a shiny surface. When they looked up, they saw the sun reflecting off of a large circular object. They estimated it to be about one hundred feet across and it looked like polished stainless steel or aluminum. It appeared to be about three miles away from where they were fishing and about three hundred to five hundred feet above the marsh. The object started to move slowly to the south until it was almost out of sight and then it slowly moved forward, toward the north, when, suddenly, it took off at a high rate of speed headed northwest. No sound was heard coming from the object. The sighting lasted about ten minutes. Shortly after the object was out of sight, two black helicopters with no markings came into the area where the lights had been.

November 22, 2003, at 5 a.m.: Two witnesses observed several white circular lights clustered together in the early morning sky. The lights were over the ocean at Murrells Inlet. The lights would appear in one location, fade out, and then reappear in another location. The sky was clear with the stars visible everywhere. You could easily distinguish the lights from the stars or planets. The lights did not act like any conventional aircraft. The witness observed these lights for about fifteen minutes.

July 28, 2004: An unidentified witness observed eight orange-red lights over Murrells Inlet. The witness reported there were four horizontal and two sets of two vertical lights about ten degrees above the horizon and about two miles from the shore. First, one light appeared in the sky, and then another one appeared above the first light. The lights lasted between fifteen and thirty seconds and then went out. About three minutes later, a second light appeared to the south of the first lights; then a second light appeared over that light. About three minutes later, a third set of lights appeared. This time there were four lights in a horizontal line. The lights were equal distance from each other. All four lights illuminated at the same time and vanished at the same time.

July 29, 2004: A single witness observed bright orange lights over the ocean at Murrells Inlet, South Carolina. The witness was a 54-year-old grandmother enjoying a trip to the beach with her grandchildren. She was standing on the balcony of her twelfth floor condo when she first spotted the lights. There was no streaming light, like from a flare, and no sound or smoke. Five minutes later, another orange light appeared to the right of where the first one appeared, and then three more orange lights appeared at the same time. They then just went out. A single light appeared and then disappeared. The lights did not fade out…they just disappeared.

February 20, 2005: A number of people were on a boat on the Intercoastal Waterway cat fishing. The sky was clear and visibility was unlimited. The witness was looking for shooting stars when two objects were observed moving across the sky. The objects were very high and were moving very fast. The objects headed north and abruptly turned directions, then went almost in a reversed direction. No noise could be heard from the objects and there were no blinking lights. The lights were very bright compared to the brightness of the stars. The objects appeared to be precise in their direction and movement. After about forty minutes, the objects went north and out of sight.

April 20, 2006, at 3 p.m.: An unidentified witness reported that he was boarding his boat in the Intercoastal Waterway in Murrells Inlet, South Carolina, when he spotted an octagon-shaped UFO with dings in the exterior of the craft. It also had green tarnish marks on the outside. The UFO was five hundred feet to one mile away from the witness. The octagon-shaped UFO was hovering and bouncing like a dragonfly. After about five seconds, it moved up the Intercoastal Waterway towards Wilmington, North Carolina. Shortly after, another one appeared in the exact location. It remained there for about the same amount of time as the first one did and then shot off into space. The one that went up the river shot off into space also. The witness reported that he didn't know how he got close enough to the UFO to see the dings and tarnish marks. The witness reported that he never moved, but could see himself standing on the dock looking to his right, and then he came down and circled back into his body on the left side. The craft looked almost ancient and alive.

May 25, 2006, at 3:30 p.m.: The witness was getting on his sailboat at the Waccawatche Marina in Murrells Inlet when he looked toward the west and noticed an octagon-shaped craft flying up the Iintercoastal Waterway. It was there for about five seconds and then disappeared. The witness described it as being octagon-shaped and looked like something from late

BC or early AD. As soon as the first craft disappeared, another one appeared in the exact location where the first craft was first spotted. The craft was about four hundred yards away from the witness. The witness reported he was close enough to see that it was bronze in color with tarnish marks and had little dings in it. He also noticed dark windows in the craft. He reported, "How I got close enough to see this I have no idea...even though I do remember seeing myself over my left shoulder standing on the dock and re-entering myself. I am still watching this thing." The craft continued to hover over the Intercoastal Waterway like a dragonfly. The bottom of the craft turned to molten lava like it was in a glass bowl. The craft did two giant loops and then headed off to the south. It left a green trail behind it. The sighting lasted for about two minutes.

June 28, 2007, at 11 p.m.: Two orange lights appeared just above the ocean and seemed to fade in and out. They reappeared about fifteen minutes later in the same area. The witness walked over the dunes to the ocean and saw other strange clusters of orange lights in different locations throughout the sky. They were much smaller than the first lights and would pulse sometimes in a diagonal pattern. Some of the lights seemed to move around while others remained motionless. The orange lights reappeared about thirty to forty minutes later. This time there was a very distinct pattern when the lights pulsed. There were six to eight lights in each group. There seemed to be a big decrease in the temperature of the breeze blowing in off the ocean while the lights were there. The activity of the last lights lasted about ten minutes. The witness reported that there were other witnesses and that they had seen the lights three nights in a row.

October 16, 2008, at 11 p.m.: As the witness was leaving work, the witness noticed an orange light in the sky over the Atlantic Ocean. The weather was clear with no clouds in the sky and the stars were clearly visible. The light moved slowly from the witness's left to right and then disappeared. The orange light reappeared in a different location and then shortly after was joined by two more lights. All three lights disappeared at the same time and did not reappear again.

April 17, 2009, at 10 p.m.: A UFO was observed over the ocean at Murrells Inlet, South Carolina. The witnesses believed the UFO was about 2,000 to 5,000 feet above the water. The witnesses first observed a bright flash of light that brought the UFO to their attention. There were three pulses of dim yellow light observed. The light grew rapidly in intensity, dimmed just as rapidly, and then reappeared within a second. The three lights appeared to be on the same object, but continued to dim at different intervals. The UFO moved farther out to sea. The lights flashed one more time before the UFO moved out of sight.

July 28, 2009, no time given except that it was at night: A flying object was seen hovering over the ocean at Murrells Inlet for about ten seconds. The lights were yellowish-orange to completely white. There were five lights and they seemed to pulsate in order. The lights were much brighter than the stars in the background. The object appeared to be between three hundred and five hundred feet above the ocean. The lights disappeared after about ten seconds.

June 5, 2011: A family was vacationing in Murrells Inlet when they spotted some unusual lights in the sky. They were on the third-floor balcony of their condo building when they witnessed the lights out over the ocean. The lights would get into a triangle and then disappear. The lights would show up a few seconds later miles away from where they were first witnessed. A burning red-colored light then streaked away, leaving a red trail behind. After about fifteen minutes, the lights reappeared again to the right of the condo. This time, there was an oval-shaped craft with fixed lights around it. The objects, including the oval-shaped one, disappeared as quickly as they appeared. They also witnessed a craft spinning at a slant going into the ocean, and then another craft took off upward and out of sight. The light show lasted for about thirty minutes.

September 11, 2012: The witness stated that he was at a festival in Murrells Inlet when he witnessed the strange lights. The orange circular lights appeared one at a time, with a third one forming a triangle. The lights then disappeared. A few minutes later another light appeared, faded away, and then reappeared in a different location and faded out. The witness reported that many people witnessed this. He reported that one lady caught it on film. The witness left a name and phone number on his report, but, when I tried to contact him, he would answer the phone and then hang up. He did not return my call when I left a message.

September 12, 2012, at 10 p.m.: Lights were reported over the ocean in Murrells Inlet. The witness was sitting on the porch when what was believed to be a shooting star was observed. The witness reported there was no trail left behind the light. About fifteen minutes later, in the same direction, the witness observed two lights hovering in the night sky, then a third one appeared, and then a fourth one. The first lights faded out of sight, then the other lights faded and were gone. The lights did not reappear.

September 12, 2012, 10:15 p.m.: Three people witnessed strange lights in the sky over Murrells Inlet. The lights appeared twice for a period of about twenty seconds during a twenty-minute period. This is the description given by the witnesses: Three lights appeared in the night sky and then V-shaped lights pointing towards the lights. The lights started going out one at a time. When all of the lights had gone out, the V-shaped lights, still pointing in the same direction, started moving in a north to south direction. The V-shape moved out of sight.

September 13, 2012, at 6:49 p.m.: The weather was fantastic in Murrells Inlet, South Carolina, so some friends were enjoying their boat in the creek. The friends saw some lights standing vertically and moving to their left about one-half mile away. The lights were bright, glowing yellow-orange, and then all of a sudden the lights went out completely. The lights returned over Garden City, South Carolina, in front of the Gulf Stream Café. Now there were two lights very close together, then one light went out. The other light flickered out. The lights reappeared at a different location and then moved rapidly back to the original location. Eight to ten lights then came on and formed a circle. The lights rotated several times and then they got smaller, formed a straight line, and vanished.

ST. STEPHEN

I kept getting reports of UFOs over St. Stephen, but nobody would come forth for an interview. No newspapers or TV stations had carried any stories on the St. Stephen UFO wave, though the Internet was full of them. None had any names attached to them, and all told the same information in two or three lines…or maybe some information had been deleted before being posted.

On Saturday, March 3rd, I received an e-mail from Will Finch. It was two pages long and had the name and phone number of an eyewitness to the St. Stephen UFOs. It was Milton Finch, Will Finch's brother, and on March 5th I called Milton Finch. Finch was very interested in giving an interview. I did a follow-up interview with him on March 8th. The following is the e-mail and interview combined into one.

My father and mother taught me at a young age to enjoy the created order of nature. I have always enjoyed looking and studying those things, including the heavens. I love a starry night. Sometimes it seems that you can see forever.

Things became a lot more interesting on the night of August 29th, 2011. My wife, Audrey, enjoys sky watching as much as I do. We were out looking at the starry sky between 9 and 10 p.m. that night.

We are located on the south side of St. Stephen and we were looking in a northerly direction. We saw a group of four lights coming from the northwest that seemed to be above Lake Moultrie. The lights were heading in our direction. The lights were always white and blinked with no rhythm. When they seemed to get above St. Stephen, two split off from the group and headed a little farther toward the east. The two that stayed behind seemed to remain motionless and just seemed to hover over the town of St. Stephen.

We have two main arteries of travel in our area: One is to the east that goes from south to north-northeast and the other one comes at a slant going from our south-southwest to the north-northeast, which would be slightly to our west. There is an area in the sky between these areas that gets very little air traffic.

What we noticed was that the two lights that were above the town would go up to each commercial jet coming in from both sides from our west, span it, and yet remain in a lower altitude than the plane. They appeared to be gauging the altitudes of these commercial planes and then they would return to a lower level above St. Stephen. The other two lights were doing the same thing to the commercial air traffic to our east. There was no sound, no vapor trail, nor smoke from any of these lights. The lights didn't make any movement toward the planes.

This pattern continued for about twenty minutes as the blinking lights seemed to investigate five or six commercial planes. Some were to the east and others to the west; then they regrouped and headed back in the direction that they came from, which was to the north of Lake Moultrie, heading towards Santee. My wife and I thought this was very strange, but it was our first time, so we called no one.

After this incident, we always kept our eyes toward the north at night, to the area where we first saw the lights.

Milton Finch said this was not the only UFO sighting that they have witnessed.

On the night of September 29th, 2011, an even more dramatic event unfolded in the sky above St. Stephen. It was around 9:20 p.m. We were walking our dog before heading off to bed. There was no air traffic in the sky. We turned around to go into the house and I happened to look back and there were eight to ten flashing lights. We were amazed because ten seconds before there was no traffic in the sky. The lights were forming a circle. We looked at them for about two minutes. They were just sitting there. No smoke, no vapor trail, and no noise. They were just sitting there, holding the circular pattern, and then what appeared to be a meteor fell right between them. It was orange and had a tail. It appeared to be as large as your thumbnail at arm's length. When the orange object fell, the lights broke formation. Some headed to the east; four headed to the west in the same area above Lake Maultrie. We kept looking at those because we soon lost the ones heading east due to the trees.

We then heard two jets coming from Charleston Air Force Base. They were at full-throttle, heading toward the blinking objects that went to the north of Lake Maultrie. We could still hear the jets after they were out of sight. We looked back to the location where the blinking lights were and another orange fireball fell in the exact location as the first fireball fell.

The following day, I reported this to the Charleston newspaper and called the Charleston International Airport to see if they had any unusual occurrences that night. I never heard back from either of them. (Author's note: Most newspapers won't run a story on UFOs or strange lights in the sky for fear of being categorized as a tabloid. Airports or the air force never have any information on UFOs or strange lights in the sky if they return your call, which they rarely do.)

I also reported this incident to the National UFO Reporting Center. I found that there had been three other UFO sightings that night and they were in the Myrtle Beach, South Carolina, area. One of those incidents involved military jets chasing the lights.

On January 18th, at 8:15 p.m., I was out scanning the night sky again and saw five or six blinking lights that matched the first two sightings. They were heading our way. I yelled for my wife and two grown children that were visiting us to come outside.

When the lights arrived above the town of St. Stephen, they seemed to just hover there, and then all of a sudden, just a little to our northeast, appeared a perfect orange sphere in the sky. It was the size of a dime held at arm's length. It was there for two to five seconds and then disappeared as fast as it appeared. (Author's note: I am familiar with the appearing and disappearing spheres. My first encounter with them was May 5, 2009, at 8 p.m. Three gold spheres appeared and disappeared. The complete story is in my first book, *Forgotten Tales of South Carolina*.) It didn't come from any direction. It just appeared. It stayed in the same spot and then disappeared.

The blinking lights headed over to the spot where the orange sphere was last seen and remained there for about one minute, and then headed to the northeast and out of sight. Four family members witnessed this UFO incident.

On January 19th, 2012, at 11:06 p.m. we were out taking our dog for a walk and we both spotted what I can only describe as a tear or rip in the sky. I got a better look at it because I was looking in that direction when it happened. It was bright plasma green. I have seen falling stars or meteorites before and this was nothing like that. This thing came down straight. It came through the atmosphere and I could make out its loss of altitude. My wife was looking at it from a different area. As we were looking at where it went out, another orange sphere appeared. It was about the size of an aspirin at arm's length. It hovered there in the east-northeast direction for about twenty seconds. The orange light started slowly moving to the south. After about fifteen seconds, the light started pulsating. This went on for about another fifteen seconds and then it started blinking with white and red lights.

Note: Milton Finch called me several days after I interviewed him and told me that military jets were dropping flares in the vicinity of where the lights were seen. This UFO incident did attract media attention. The *Berkeley Independent* would boldly go where no other newspaper would. They ran two stories on the St. Stephen Lights. The first line in the article was "The truth is out there." Their first story was March 21, 2012.

Milton Finch, St. Stephen UFO Witness
Milton Finch was born the son of Reverend Floyd and Leona Finch on March 3, 1959, in Lenoir, North Carolina.

In his adult life, Finch has been involved in various church functions and positions. He was a lay-rector of the Cursillo movement in the Berkeley, Colleton, and Dorchester county region of the Episcopal Church in the Diocese of South Carolina. Being a devout Christian, Finch has done serious Bible study. He even wrote a book from his years of Bible study: *Hello Again, Already: A Book For the Spiritually Minded Christian.*

Finch was a volunteer with Low Country AIDS Services located in Charleston, South Carolina, from 1998 until 2003. He became involved with that after reading a book by Mother Teresa of Calcutta.

Finch also served as president of the Parent Teacher Organization at Saint Johns Christian School in Moncks Corner, South Carolina.

He is married to Audrey and has two grown children and one grandson. Finch and his wife have always been avid sky watchers, enjoying God's great creation. Finch was never interested that much in UFOs until late summer of 2011, but all of that changed after he and Audrey saw their first UFO. They now have chairs and a table set up at the side of their yard for nightly viewing — weather permitting of course — and as of March 2012, they have logged in around 350 hours of sky watching over a seven-month period. It's not like just going outside and seeing these things in the sky. It has been a serious effort on their part.

Finch said, "The amount of money spent on video equipment has been considerable in the past few months. In essence, I've grabbed the bull by the horns in my quest to find out and get it on tape what is out there in the sky over St. Stephen."

UFOS AT NUCLEAR FACILITIES, DAMS, AND POWER PLANTS

As far back as 1949, UFOs have been seen around atomic and nuclear facilities in America. Power plants and dams are no stranger to UFOs either. Incidents have occurred at these and many other sites around the country, such as the Savannah River, Hanford, Los Alamos, Oak Ridge, McGuire, Cherokee, and Indian Point. Are UFOs monitoring certain facilities?

Declassified United States government documents and testimony from more than one hundred former and retired military personnel establish beyond any doubt that UFOs are invading the air space around American nuclear weapon sites and power plants.

Nuclear missile sites have been shut down, also referred to as inoperable. Missile silos mysteriously lost electricity. The military refused to acknowledge these incidents or investigate them. Witnesses were told that it didn't happen.

Savannah River Plant / Savannah River Site

The Savannah River Plant is located in Aiken, Allendale, and Barnwell counties, adjacent to the Savannah River. It was built during the 1950s to refine nuclear material for use in nuclear weapons; the site covers 310 square miles.

The Savannah River Site is owned by the United States Department of Energy and is home to the Savannah River National Laboratory and America's only operating radiochemical separation facility. The Savannah River Site tritium facility is also the United States' only source of tritium — an essential component in nuclear weapons.

A timeline for the site's acquisition and construction of the plant is as follows:

1950-1951: The federal government contracted Dupont to build and operate a nuclear facility near the Savannah River in South Carolina. A large amount of farmland, thousands of homes and businesses, the towns of Ellenton and Dunbarton, as well as several communities (Meyers Mill, Leigh, Robbins, and Hauthorne), were brought under eminent domain. Most had nowhere to go and had to start life all over again. All they had were a few possessions and the small amount of money they were paid for their property. Some had spent a lifetime on their property, probably their parents too. Many had very little transportation to get to where they were going, but that's the government for you — they take what they want. This became the 310 square miles of the Savannah River Site, which is managed by the United States Atomic Energy Commission.

1952-1954: Production of heavy water for the reactors began and reactors R, P, L, and K went on.

On November 4, 1954, the world's first operational PUREX (plutonium and uranium extraction) separation plant began radioactive operations.

1955-1956: Reactor C went on. The first plutonium was shipped from the site.

In 1956, Fred Reines and Clyde Cowan discovered the neutrino using flux from reactor P.

1961: Professor Eugene Odum, from the University of Georgia, founded the Savannah River Ecology Laboratory to study the effects of radiation on organisms at the Savannah River Site.

1962-1964: They tested the heavy water components test reactor.

1972: The Savannah River Site was designated as a National Environmental Research Park.

1985-1987: H B line began producing plutonium 238 for NASA's deep space exploration program.

1988-1989: The Savannah River Site became regulated by the EPA. Westinghouse Savannah River Company took over management and operations.

1990-1993: With the end of the Cold War, production of nuclear materials for weapons was slowed down.

2002: Scientists reported finding a new species of radiation-resistant Extremophiles inside one of the tanks. It was named Kineococcus Radiotolerans.

2005: The tritium extraction facility was completed for the purpose of extracting tritium from materials in the Tennessee Valley Authority's commercial nuclear reactors.

2007: On August 1st, construction began on the $4.86 billion MOX facility.

Nuclear facilities are no stranger to UFO activity, as they are frequently visited by UFOs. However, the government won't admit to any visitations by UFOs.

May 10, 1952, at 10:45 p.m.: Four DuPont construction workers at the Savannah River Plant saw four disc-shaped objects approach the plant at a very low altitude. The UFOs had to go up to pass over some of the tall tanks on the plant site. The UFOs made no sound as they moved left to right and from side to side. They departed at a ninety-degree angle and were moving from south to north at a very high speed. The color of the UFOs varied from yellow to gold. The objects were seen five different times between 10:45 and 11:15 p.m.

July 28, 1952: U.S. Air Command in Washington, D.C. scrambled several F-94 fighter jets when they received reports of glowing white lights over Aiken, South Carolina.

November 24, 1952: Two heavy equipment operators reported seeing a red fireball over the Savannah River Plant. There was no trail leading from the fireball and no sound was connected to it.

Air Force reports from 1952 show officially recorded UFO sightings that could not be identified. The Air Force's position on this is that the objects were not being controlled by a reasoning being and therefore there was no threat.

November 18, 2004, at 11:30 p.m.: A silver cylindrical-shaped craft passed over the Savannah River site. The Savannah River site is about sixteen miles south of Aiken, South Carolina. The craft had no visible wings, there was no sound coming from the craft, and no visible vapor trail. The craft was flying in a straight line from northwest to southeast and had passed beneath a contrail left by a jet that had passed over minutes ago. The craft appeared to be about as high as the jet, and was about eight times as long as it was wide. No windows could be seen due to the distance from the witness. It appeared to be flying or gliding about as fast as a conventional jet. The weather conditions were clear. The craft was visible for about two minutes.

December 12, 2011, at 6 p.m.: In Aiken County, South Carolina, six hunters witnessed a group of lights descend near the ground and hover. The field the hunters were in was between six hundred and eight hundred acres. They were within sight of the Savannah River Site. The hunters watched a group of yellow lights quietly and quickly descend out of the sky and hover close to the ground for about one minute. When the object stopped descending, the lights got extremely bright. After about a minute, the lights dimmed, the object slowly ascended, and then it streaked off into the sky.

Cherokee Nuclear Station

The uncompleted Cherokee Nuclear Station was started in the early 1970s when Duke Power began work on a three reactor nuclear power plant ten miles outside of Gaffney. Many buildings were built and one reactor was partially completed when, due to economic problems, work was stopped on the reactor in 1982. After spending $633 million, Duke Power halted construction on the site completely in 1983.

Shortly after construction was stopped, Earl Owensby, a Shelby, North Carolina, businessman, converted the abandoned Cherokee nuclear power plant into a movie studio and, in 1987, Hollywood movie director James Cameron decided to use the newly-renovated Cherokee nuclear power plant facilities to film the underwater scenes for *The Abyss*, a two-hour science fiction thriller. However, more modifications to the facility had to be made before the movie company could come in and start filming. The turbine pit was modified to hold

2.2 million gallons of water. Cinematographer Al Giddings found that the turbine pit was not big enough for the film's needs. The containment vessel for the reactor, two hundred feet across and fifty-five feet deep, was converted to hold 7.5 million gallons of water. The containment vessel was used as "A" tank and the turbine pit was used as "B" tank. The cast and crew had to go through decompression due to the depth of the water and the length of time spent in it.

Interior sets were built inside nearby warehouses located on the site. In December 1988, production at the Cherokee nuclear power plant wrapped and moved back to Hollywood. The tanks were drained, but the movie sets remained on the site. Signs were placed on the structures stating that the sets remain the property of 20th Century Fox and that video photography was prohibited. In September 2007, *The Abyss* sets were destroyed. *The Abyss* broke the record for the largest underwater movie set in the world.

October 13, 1983, at 12:30 a.m.: A couple from Gaffney, South Carolina, were awakened one night by a loud noise that sounded like a siren. While searching for the source of the sound, they looked out the window just in time to see a glowing, oval-shaped object about twenty feet above one of the neighbor's houses. The witnesses described the UFO as being about twenty feet long, about ten feet high, and orange-yellow color. It emitted a high-pitched sound when it crossed the power lines. It had two lights on the bottom. The UFO moved east in the direction of the Cherokee Nuclear Station. It was visible for about five minutes.

Lake Murray Hydroelectric Plant Saluda Dam

March 1975: A couple was driving near Lake Murray Hydroelectric Plant's Saluda Dam when they witnessed a UFO. An extremely bright light suddenly illuminated the interior of their car. When they were finally able to see the source of the light, they were a little shaken. The object looked like two pie pans placed one on top of the other. The UFO had a brilliant white dome on top of it. The craft did not have any visible windows. There was no noise or smoke coming from the UFO, which flew about forty to fifty feet above their car and had red and blue lights on the bottom. The bottom of the UFO was octagonal-shaped.

CHAPTER 5

ALIEN ABDUCTIONS

There are many reports of alien abductions throughout the United States and in other countries. Here is one from 2001 in South Carolina.

A truck driver was bringing a load from North Carolina to Columbia, South Carolina, and then he had a second drop in Sumter, South Carolina. It was just another day. The driver was making good time — or so he thought. The driver was hoping for another uneventful day, but this wasn't going to be the case. This was going to be anything but an uneventful day. The driver had no idea what was in store for him. He was about to have a life-changing experience.

After making his Columbia drop with time to spare, he headed to Sumter for his last drop of the day and then home. Pushing the big rig, the driver made it home late that evening.

When retiring for bed, the driver removed his shirt and noticed in the mirror a small spot in the center of his chest that looked like a small surgical cut. This was a shocking experience since he had not had any surgery. He could not figure out where this small spot came from. He did not feel any pain associated with it, and when he touched it, it was not sore. It was just a small depression with a small incision in the center. He had never seen anything like this.

The driver had heard about people with this same type of surgical spot that had suspected they had been involved in an alien UFO abduction. The driver had seen several UFOs in the past year during his many hours on the highway, but never thought much about them. The driver began to wonder if he had been abducted and had no memory of it. In many of the abduction cases, the abductees have no memory of anything that happened.

After close examination of the incision, he thought it may have been done with a laser. The more he looked at it, the more he thought he had been abducted by aliens or somebody had performed the surgery on him and erased his memory. The driver tried to recreate the events of the day, but he couldn't remember anything that happened of that entire day. He took several pictures of the small depression, not knowing if any would turn out usable. Feeling an overwhelming desire to go to sleep, the driver put the camera down and went to bed and instantly fell asleep. It was a restless sleep.

The next morning, the driver noticed the depression was still there, but it was almost completely healed. He went to work as usual and had a normal day. When returning home that evening, he removed his shirt and noticed that the depression had completely healed — not a sign of it was left. Still, none of his memory of that day had returned.

Several days later, he found a shirt with a hole about the size of a pencil in the center of the chest. Thinking the shirt could not be repaired, he threw it away. When he got the pictures back, only two were any good. They showed the depression, but not the incision. The driver, thinking about how long it took the surgery to heal from that morning, would probably place him between Columbia and Sumter, South Carolina.

Columbia is home to Fort Jackson Army Base. Sumter is home to Shaw Air Force Base. Was the surgery done by alien beings or a secret military group? After reviewing the truck log book, it showed one hundred more miles on the truck than should have been for that trip. Wonder how many miles he was from Shaw Air Force Base or Fort Jackson?

Georgetown UFO Abduction

No exact location is given for this incident, except for down a dirt road in a rural area near Georgetown, South Carolina. Details for this incident are sketchy at best. Some local people have reported seeing a ball of light in the area. Four people — names or descriptions are not given — decided to go check it out. They took three video cameras in case they encountered the light.

As the group of people moved cautiously down the dirt road, not knowing what to expect, they had all three video cameras recording in anticipation of capturing the ball of light on film. When traveling down the dirt road, they noticed a small light approaching them. It was faint in the distance. At its closest point to them, the ball of light appeared to be about four feet across. The report states that several hours later they woke up on the road to Myrtle Beach, where they were staying. They had no memory of what happened from the time they saw the ball of light until they woke up in another location. Hours of video were missing on all three cameras. No one has been able to explain that.

The next day, one member of the group found a foreign object embedded in his hand. When he consulted a doctor about it, the doctor explained it was heated aspartame from the diet cola he had previously drank. The report stated that another one of the group had found a foreign object embedded in them also, but there is no other information about that. There are no reports of any other people having any unusual experiences when witnessing the ball of light.

I contacted MUFON, but did not get any information. There are several things with this case that are consistent with other UFO abductions: 1. Lost time; 2. Missing video footage; and 3. Foreign objects in their bodies.

Charleston UFO Abduction

Charleston, South Carolina, was once a hotbed for UFO activity. Charleston is still visited by UFOs on a frequent basis. Photos taken during daylight hours showing UFOs in restricted air space around Charleston Air Force Base were shown to Air Force personnel. The Air Force's response included "it's military planes or just forget about it."

The names in the following story have been changed to protect the abductee and his family. The only date given was 1978. The location was Charleston, South Carolina. No other details are given on the exact location. I contacted MUFON about this, but got no response. The story goes as follows:

Mr. Jones was in his backyard looking at a mysterious light in the sky. These lights were not uncommon in the area and most people paid them little to no attention. Most people don't want to believe that we're being visited by intelligent beings from somewhere else. For Mr. Jones, that night was not going to be just another night. His life would change.

Mr. Jones would wake up four hours later fifteen miles away from his home on a lonely dirt road. He would flag a passing motorist down and catch a ride back home. He contacted the Sheriff's Department to file a report.

Later, Mr. Jones was contacted by a person claiming to be Tom Olsen. They visited the site where Mr. Jones appeared on the dirt road. He took Mr. Jones back to a hotel room, where he convinced him to take a polygraph test. After the test, he took Mr. Jones home. Several weeks later, Mr. Jones tried to contact Tom Olsen — only to learn that there was a Tom Olsen, but he had never contacted Mr. Jones or heard of the abduction case.

Mr. Jones later agreed to be hypnotized by a UFO investigator from the Aerial Phenomena Research Organization. Under hypnosis, Mr. Jones revealed that he was on a large table being examined by three humanoid beings. The beings were about four feet tall, thin, pale skin, large hairless heads, and large black eyes. One of the beings spoke to Mr. Jones, but its mouth never moved. It was more like mental telepathy. It warned him that our violent nature would eventually destroy the human race. Over a period of time, Mr. Jones received messages from the beings. In May 1979, Mr. Jones claimed to have had his last contact with the alien beings.

The modern era of alien abductions began one September night in 1961 when Betty and Barney Hill were driving home to New Hampshire. The Hills saw a bright light that followed them. Barney got out of the car to get a better view of the craft. The next thing they remember was being in the car again. Fifty years later...and no one has been able to break their story.

Some scientists question whether alien abduction is real or a dream. Some believe it is sleep paralysis or just an over-active imagination. They would like for you to think that. Today, as previously noted, most alien abductions are not reported for several reasons. It can expose the abductees to public ridicule, loss of friends, loss of job, threats from the men in black or government officials, or many times they are simply labeled as a basket case.

Are these strange visitors beings from another planet, time-traveling humans from the future disguised to keep their identity a secret, or beings from another dimension?

Child Abduction

This information was found on the Internet. How factual this is remains questionable. It's the case of the alien abduction of a Greenville child. Due to the age of the child, the child's name and age, as well as the exact location of the incident, have been left out.

In the summer of (year left out), the child first reported that she had been abducted by the gray aliens. During her first abduction, she was removed from the bed — not her physical body. She felt it was her spirit being removed. She could look down on the bed and see her body, but she was not afraid of what was happening. She went with the short gray aliens to their alien station. They operated on her eye so they could scan it and identify her when she goes with them and she would be able to enter the station. She goes monthly to the alien station to help teach the alien hybrids how to learn. She said there is a part of the station where the babies are kept in a tube like water balloons hanging from the ceiling. The babies were half human and half alien hybrids. She also explained that she was there to teach them how to act like humans. At one time, the mother of the child was awakened by a bright light in her room. She rose up just in time to see a small gray figure walk through the wall. The alien communicated with her by mental telepathy and told her everything was all right and to go back to sleep. That is all she remembered of that night. When the child is on the planet, she wears a helmet hooked to a system so she can breathe earth oxygen. Their training room is a dome-type building. She doesn't have to wear the helmet in there because the aliens are learning to breathe oxygen. These abductions have been happening for five years.

UFOS FOLLOW CARS IN GREENVILLE

Many people in South Carolina and other states are afraid to report UFO sightings for fear that someone might want to ship them off to the state-giggling hospital. What happens when you have more than just a sighting, though? The following accounts are from Greenville, South Carolina.

July 9, 2008, at 10:15 p.m.: On Highway 14 near Greenville, a motorist is shaken up by a UFO hovering on his car. The witness reported he was driving home from night school and headed north when he noticed some unusual lights over the trees in the northwestern sky. When the witness got a better view of the lights, he could tell it was a dark metallic-looking triangle with three white lights and one red light. The craft seemed to be wobbling a little and then something unusual happened. There was an unnatural glow around the car. The UFO was now about five hundred feet above the car — it was completely silent and there was no smoke or contrail behind it. The witness also reported smelling something like sulfur. The witness travels this road regularly and has never smelled this before. The witness was trying to watch the road and the UFO, but when he looked up again the UFO was gone.

September 7, 2011: A South Carolina resident witnessed a UFO on Highway 278, near Wooden Horse Run intersection, in Jasper County. The witness, who was alone at the time, reported a large, unidentified craft of unknown origin hovering in front of her car. The UFO had an undetermined number of white lights on it. After hovering for a moment, it took off at a high rate of speed. Seconds later, it was again visible for a few moments through the trees on the other side of the road.

This is not uncommon in this area. Other UFOs have been reported being seen in the area. Another incident was reported, in which the car was followed by the UFO. It was reported to be a similar object.

Teenagers Chased

This next report is a little unusual:

A bright light chased the car of two teenagers on a date. They were on Fork Shoals Road, near Greenville, South Carolina, when the first incident happened. They were heading home when the light appeared behind the vehicle they were driving. The light was so bright that the driver could hardly see to drive. No matter how fast they drove the light remained the same distance behind them. They reached seventy miles an hour, but could not get away from the light. After about five minutes, the light just disappeared. This happened on October 4, 1972, at approximately 10 p.m.

In 1999 (no other date or time given), they were driving from Florence to Georgetown. They had just finished eating supper and pulled out onto Highway 20, leaving Florence. They stopped at a red light with other cars when all of a sudden a bright, white-bluish light appeared behind them. At first they thought it was a police car so they started to pull over when the light vanished. The other cars on the road had vanished. There was nothing on the road except them — everything had vanished.

Also in 1972, on May 11th or June 1st (there were two different dates on the report) at 9:30 p.m., a single witness observed a strange moving craft in the sky above Greenville. The witness was visiting relatives when the sighting occurred. The witness pulled off the road into a clearing near where his cousin's mobile home was located. When the car stopped, the witness observed a green light moving vertically to treetop level. It seemed to just float up and stop. It remained motionless for several seconds and then moved off to the left very fast. The object then came to a sudden stop and just floated up again. The object did this three more times until it was directly over the car, but when the witness got out of the car and looked up there was nothing there. The object was gone. The object was described as a bright green circle with no noise or trail behind it.

Other Greenville UFO Reports

August 10, 1974, at about 6 p.m.: Just outside of Greenville, two witnesses observed three rectangular objects hovering over an open field. The reporting witness and his girlfriend were on their way to church when they witnessed the UFOs. They were approximately two miles down Woodruff Road, headed towards Mauldin, South Carolina. They spotted a line of cars parked on the side of the road. They parked their car and walked over to where the people were. They were looking at a rectangular object about three hundred to five hundred feet above an open field. It was on the left side of the road. The reporting witness estimated the UFO was about 2,500 to 3,000 feet long. There was a low humming sound coming from the UFO. All of a sudden two smaller UFOs appeared, one on each side of the larger UFO. All three had a contentious stream of red and white lights going around the outside edge of them. The reporting witness said the top of the UFO looked kind of like the top of a battleship. All three UFOs left at the same time.

March 21, 1993, at 9:30 p.m.: Two witnesses were in the parking lot going to work when they noticed two objects in the sky. At first they thought they were meteorites, but soon realized that the lights were coming down too uniformly and were not burning out or leaving a trail behind them (the witness refers to the lights as burns). At first there were two burns; then seconds later a third burn was observed. They didn't look exactly like lights. They looked more like a friction burn. The three burns outlined a huge dark triangle object against the starry night sky. The witnesses were heading to work and couldn't wait to see what the object was going to do. One of the witnesses called the local TV station and inquired about the lights and was told they were meteors.

December 28, 2000, at 11 p.m.: A man was standing on his deck looking into the clear night sky when he noticed something that appeared to be a very bright star. After a few seconds, he could tell that it was moving in a westerly direction. After a few minutes the light stopped. He went inside to get his wife, but when they returned the light was gone.

Thanksgiving Day, November 22, 2001: For about thirty minutes fireballs lit up and performed in the night sky for a group of onlookers. Two people were traveling southbound on Interstate 85 heading to Iva, South Carolina, when they noticed cars parked on the side of the road. At this time they saw two or three fireballs in the sky. At first, they thought it might be some kind of airplane, but the fireballs continued to appear — more than fifty — in the night sky. Some of the fireballs were moving in all directions, others were stationary. They would go from side to side or up and down. The fireballs were small and, though they covered the horizon, none of them were seen hitting the ground.

April 28, 2003, at 10:10 p.m.: Two brothers from Greenville were outside doing a little stargazing when they noticed three stars in a triangular formation. They were spread out, not attached to one another. All three were moving at the same speed and direction. They were moving at about the same speed as a satellite. They appeared to be out of the earth's atmosphere because the sun was reflecting off of them. As they watched, the lights moved past the horizon and out of sight. This lasted for about one minute.

August 23, 2004, at 11:10 p.m.: White lights were observed by a single motorist on Interstate 85. The motorist was heading east when he observed four white lights that were about one and one half times as bright as Venus. The lights were in a straight line. Another white light was centered at the back of the other lights. This one was about the size of the moon. In the middle of the lights was a red light. The red light was brighter than the white ones. At one time they appeared to be stationary for about forty-five seconds. The driver turned around at the next exit and went back, looking for a safe place to pull off the road and watch the lights. The lights were now traveling parallel to Interstate 85. The driver continued to watch as he drove. The lights went behind a cloud and did not reappear. This sighting was near Greenville and lasted for about six minutes.

October 23, 2004, at 5 a.m.: A boy and his girlfriend were driving home and, as they neared Greenville, they noticed two lights in the sky at about a forty-five degree angle. The lights just hovered with no motion. They were about thirty minutes from home at the time of the sighting. The lights were still visible when they arrived home and were still hovering in the same place. The boy stayed up until about 6:30. Just before going to bed he went back outside to look again. The lights were still there. He reported that several of his friends saw the lights in the same location several nights before. The boy reported that he had some strange experiences that morning in the living room. He said that it seemed like several dimensions were opening at the same time. He saw a man in the kitchen, another man standing by the television, and one came through the front door. This is all the information that was available.

June 10, 2005, at about 4 p.m.: This report was made two years after the sighting on January 19, 2007. The witness said the reason she hesitated to file a report was due to being from South Carolina, where the people are not open-minded about things like this. The sighting occurred near Greenville and lasted for about ten minutes. The weather was not too sunny, but not heavily overcast either. She was at home with her husband, daughter, and roommate. Her husband had stepped out onto the porch and she followed him outside. They were looking at some birds flying over the treetops about two hundred yards away when she noticed a shiny metal object resembling a saucer. It looked to be about as high as a small plane flies. The object was just hovering and not making any sound. After a few seconds it started spinning at alternating speeds. It looked like it was spinning in all directions, and the shape of the object was changing with every spin. It would move in a different direction, hover for a few seconds, and then move up or down and hover again. After about ten minutes, it slowly moved toward the west and out of sight. It did not scare the birds at all.

January 25, 2007: Fox Carolina News reported blue and green lights were spotted in the night sky around eight o'clock that night. WYFF Channel 4 news reported that viewers were calling in, reporting blue and green lights in the sky about 8:15 p.m. The Sheriff's offices in Greenville and Pickens counties also reported calls coming in about the blue and green lights. No one was able to explain what the lights were. WYFF Chief Meteorologist reports that most likely it was a group of meteors coming into the earth's atmosphere. The color could be an indication of the composition of the meteors.

August 13, 2009, at about 1 a.m.: The witness was on top of his house waiting on a meteor shower when the sky began to get cloudy. The meteor shower was supposed to start around 2 a.m., but with the clouds moving in it was unlikely that the meteor shower would be visible. However, like any diehard meteor fan, the roof sitter remained. At about 1:26 a.m., the witness observed a strange cigar-shaped craft moving into view. The craft was low and completely silent. It had two white lights on the front. The front was a little wider than the rest of the craft. It had three small lights down the side that were visible to the viewer. These three lights would blink on and off in a pattern. The light would fade out as the next one would come on. The craft slowly moved over the treetops and out of sight.

October 1, 2011, at 11 p.m.: Three people witnessed multiple lights in the sky near Greenville. The mother spotted the lights first and called them to the attention of the others. There were two lights blinking in the sky: one was red-blue and one was red. They were blinking in a sporadic manner. The lights were stationary and no sound could be heard. When they viewed the lights through binoculars, the lights appeared to be moving in a circular motion. This lasted for about fifteen minutes.

GAFFNEY'S CELESTIAL VISITOR

    Gaffney, South Carolina, has made the news more times than any other city in the Palmetto State for important UFO sightings. One of the more famous ones was the UFO crash of February 4, 2004. I wrote a story on the crash in my first book *Forgotten Tales of South Carolina*. I was contacted by a publisher that wanted me to write a book on South Carolina UFOs and, while doing more research on the Gaffney UFO crash, I ran into a lot of "I'm not going to get contacted back." I contacted the *Gaffney Ledger* newspaper, the Gaffney Police Department, the South Carolina MUFON director, the Cherokee Sheriff's Department, the Corinth Fire Department, and MUFON headquarters. The only response I received was from MUFON, stating: "At this time we have nothing in our database for that time and location." I went back to the computer to do a search for the information that I used for the first story — the websites were gone.

But Gaffney was making UFO news decades before February 2004.

Around 4 a.m. on the morning of November 17, 1966, Gaffney, South Carolina, would make UFO history. November 16-17th, the Leonid meteor shower was lighting up the sky with heavenly fire. Millions of people spent the nights outside watching the sky light up with a dazzling display of celestial fireworks. UFO offices and researchers were braced for a flood of UFO reports, as many people mistake a meteor for a UFO.

Only one report of a UFO sighting came in, though, and that was an unusual sighting. It was also one to be taken seriously due to the credibility of the two witnesses — it was a report from two policemen from South Carolina. The names of the officers have been left out since I was unable to contact them. The two policemen were on routine patrol around Gaffney at around 4 a.m. on a lonely stretch of road…an isolated and unpopulated road in an outlying part of Gaffney known locally as the West Buford Street extension. They rounded a bend in the road and observed a circular metallic craft descending directly in front of them. The craft appeared to be about twenty feet above the ground when they first encountered it.

It was described as being spherical with a flat rim around it. There were no windows or lights visible on the craft. As the craft continued to descend, the two officers sat there in silence. It stopped a few feet from the ground. No landing gear was seen on the craft. It seemed to just hover there. The policemen got out of their patrol car, but continued to stand near the car and just watch the craft. They watched as a small door opened and a ladder dropped down. They could not see anything inside the craft due to the brightness of the light inside.

A small being about the size of a twelve-year-old boy with an almost human face descended the steps. The being did not wear a helmet or any other head gear. It was dressed in a shiny gold, almost metallic-looking, one-piece suit. The being did most of the talking. When the officers asked it a question, they got no answer. The being just continued to talk. The being did not make any sudden moves. It just stood there and continued to talk. The being pronounced every word very precisely. The officers did not detect an accent.

The entire encounter with the strange being was about two to three minutes long. The being moved slowly backwards and entered the craft. The craft then slowly lifted into the night sky and vanished in the distance.

The policemen reported this unusual incident to the chief and made their usual reports. Somehow the story leaked out, but did not get reported outside of Gaffney. The next day, they returned to the landing site with one of the councilmen and found small footprints in the area where the being was standing.

Several weeks later, two men showed up in Gaffney, made a few inquiries and phone calls, and after the policemen didn't want to talk to them they left town.

Other Gaffney UFO Reports

January 19, 1973, at 11:25 p.m.: A Cherokee County youth observed a landed UFO with about twelve UFO occupants (ufonauts) about thirteen miles from Gaffney, South Carolina.

The youth was traveling south on South Carolina Highway 18 and was about thirteen miles south of Gaffney when he saw something flashing up ahead in the road. He saw some flashing lights of different colors. Thinking it may be a wreck and the lights were from emergency vehicles, he slowed down and was prepared to pull off onto the side of the road. As he got closer to the scene, though, he could see there was no accident. He saw a domed saucer-shaped object sitting in the middle of the road with the lights coming from around the base of the dome. There were red, blue, green, and white flashing lights. They were flashing in no particular order.

The craft was surrounded by about twelve beings, each wearing white coveralls. The beings were average height, with black hair, and the skin was the color of a Caucasian's — at least the best he could tell with the available lights: the dark yellow glow from the craft and the headlights from his car.

The craft was supported on three legs with the ladder coming down on the opposite side of the craft. The youth could not see inside the craft. The beings did nothing but stand near the craft. Those with their backs turned towards him looked around, but none showed any particular interest in him or the car. The beings appeared to waver much like a person looks when they are viewed through heat radiating from some source.

There were no windows in the craft. The only opening he saw was the one with the ladder. He said the craft covered about three-fourths of the highway, which would have been about fifteen feet in diameter. The highway pavement measures about twenty-two feet across in that area, according to state highway department figures. The height of the craft was about fifteen feet. There was no physical evidence left at the landing site. This could be because the craft landed on the highway pavement.

Several other witnesses reported seeing strange lights in the sky in the same area during that week.

The most controversial UFO sightings are of UFO occupants on the ground, as the previous report might indicate. Encounters of this type have been reported in twelve states: Dobson and Copeland, North Carolina; Gaffney, South Carolina; Robesonia, Pennsylvania; Balls Ferry and Chatswort, California; Athens and Danielsville, Georgia; Giles County and Watauga, Tennessee; Pascagoula, Mississippi; Falkville, Alabama; Danville, Virginia; Hampton, New Hampshire; Pensacola, Florida; and Baltimore, Maryland. Most reports describe the occupants as about four feet tall and wearing coveralls.

October 13, 1983, at about 12:30 a.m.: Mr. and Mrs. Roop (name changed) had settled in for a good night's sleep, but that wasn't going to happen. At about 12:30 a.m., the couple was awakened by what sounded like a siren or something taking off. They rushed to the window in time to see a glowing, oval-shaped UFO above their neighbor's house. They described the UFO as about as big as a Winnebago. There were two beams of light coming from the bottom of the UFO. The UFO was orange-yellow in color and emitted a high-pitched sound as it crossed the power lines and headed east in the direction of the Cherokee Nuclear Station. They estimated the UFO to be about twenty feet long and ten feet high. The UFO was not moving very fast, so they got to watch it for about five minutes.

June 12, 1991, at 6 a.m.: A truck driver was traveling near Gaffney, South Carolina. The sun was coming up. "Another perfect sunrise," he thought. The driver looked ahead and spotted a triangle-shaped object; the object was moving about thirty miles an hour and was headed towards the driver. The triangle stopped about one-fourth of a mile away and just hovered there. The object was about sixty feet long and thirty feet wide, very shiny, and had no windows. The sun was coming up behind the driver and reflecting off of the craft, so he couldn't tell the exact color. The craft started to slowly disappear — the witness said he could see the heat coming off the craft as it disappeared.

February 24, somewhere between 8:30 and 9:30 p.m.: The witnesses were standing in their yard, looking at what they thought was Venus. It was stationary for a few minutes and then it started to move. As it moved closer, it started to emit large sparks. The light appeared to be about the size of a large car. It was a yellowish-white colored ball of light. It was about fifty feet high and started to wobble a little. It made no noise. It suddenly sped up and changed directions; now it was going toward the north. Sparks were still dropping from it as far as the witness could see.

June 5, 2004, at 8 p.m.: Three people witnessed a strange fireball in the sky near Gaffney. The first witness was in his yard when he noticed a yellowish fireball that appeared to be sparkling. The witness, thinking it was too early for Fourth of July fireworks since it was still a month away, called to his father. His father was also outside, but had not seen the fireball. He pointed out the fireball to his father and then called to his mother to bring the camera. His mother came out, but without the camera. The three of them watched the strange fireball start moving toward Interstate 85. It continued to slowly move north, and when it was about one mile past the witness's house, it shot off to the north very quickly.

November 2, 2006, at 8 p.m.: The witness was driving to Gastonia, North Carolina, and was at Exit 100 on Interstate 85 when he noticed two very bright stars. These stars were much brighter than the other stars. The two stars were not flickering like the other stars were and were in a straight line, one above the other. The top light started to flicker and disappeared. About fifteen seconds later, the bottom light flickered and disappeared.

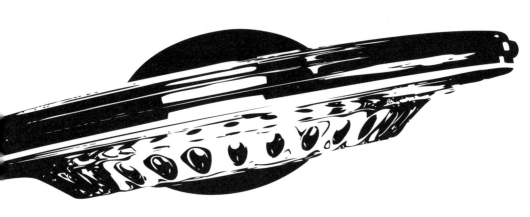

MYRTLE BEACH

Exploding UFO

Many UFO sightings have been reported along the Grand Strand of Myrtle Beach, South Carolina. Many different shapes, sizes, and colors of lights have been reported over the years, but this next report stands out, as several witnesses reported the UFO to the local police department and Myrtle Beach Air Force Base. The Air Force said they were not conducting any training exercises on the night of the sighting.

Lynne Ebert of Socastee, South Carolina, was one of the witnesses to this unusual UFO sighting. She was out walking her dog and was standing in front of her house, looking up at the sky. It was a clear night with the stars visible all around. She spotted the big dipper and then she started looking for the little dipper. As she was looking across the starlit sky, she noticed a star that was much bigger than the others and was twinkling. As she continued to watch this unusual star, it started getting closer and bigger. All of a sudden it looked like it exploded — it went in all directions. What Ebert thought exploded was still there, though. The object started moving to her left very fast and then came to a sudden stop. It then went straight up and out of sight.

Interview with Lynne Ebert

Here is an interview with Lynne Ebert that I did for "A Storied Journey through South Carolina's Mysterious Past."

"My father was stationed here when I was born, and when he retired from the Air Force, he moved back to Myrtle Beach, South Carolina, to make it his home and raise his family. One of the first things he did was to purchase three lots in this subdivision. Twenty years ago it was a brand-new subdivision and had maybe twenty homes in it. Now there's probably two hundred in here. Myrtle Beach has grown a lot.

"A very unique experience happened to me one night while I was walking my dog for her final outing. This experience has stayed with me just like it was yesterday. I was standing about here (standing in front of her house), looking up at the sky, just staring at the stars, looking for the big dipper actually. I spotted that fairly quickly, then I started looking for the little dipper. As I was gazing across the night sky, I saw this one star that was just huge, and as I gazed at it, I noticed it was twinkling. As I stood here gazing at this huge star, it seemed to be getting closer and bigger. I remember thinking, 'Wow, I can almost reach up and touch it.' As I was standing there staring at it, it exploded. It went in every direction, but the star or what I thought was a star just stayed there. I thought that was pretty bizarre. I started yelling at my husband to come outside and screamed: 'I just saw an exploding star!' Then I saw the same center of what I thought was a star suddenly move left at a very fast rate of speed and stop. I knew it couldn't have been an airplane or helicopter or anything like that. Then it shot straight up into the air and out of sight.

"I was so excited that I ran into the house and told my family about it. My husband just played it off. I can't be the only one who saw it, I thought, and I called the Air Force base. My dad still had friends that were stationed there. I contacted one of them and told him what I had seen. He assured me that the military was not doing any training exercise that night or in the area."

Myrtle Beach Glow

About ten years ago in September, Mark Watkins was fishing in the lake on the old Myrtle Beach Air Force Base. The sun had gone down and just a few pastel colors streaked the sky. The moon had just started coming up over the treetops.

Just above the trees Watkins saw a greenish-yellow glow that was brighter than the moon or the remains of the sun. It was brighter and a different color than the few low-hanging clouds. The glow stayed above the treetops and in the same location and at the same brightness for about fifteen minutes. It was still brighter than the moon when it was completely up over the trees. The sun was too low for it to be hitting a cloud formation.

Watkins has lived in Myrtle Beach all his life and had never seen anything like that before, nor had any of the people Watkins questioned about it.

Interview with Mark Watkins
Here is an interview with Mark Watkins that I did for "A Storied Journey Through South Carolina's Mysterious Past."

"Hi, my name's Mark Watkins and I'm here at the lake on the old Myrtle Beach, South Carolina, Air Force Base. About nine or ten years ago, in I believe it was September, I was fishing out here at about dusk. The sun had already gone down and the moon was starting to come up above this tree line (pointing toward the trees). I saw a greenish-yellow glow that was brighter than the moon. It was brighter than all the other clouds. It stayed above the tree line and didn't move positions or anything. It stayed there for about ten or fifteen minutes and stayed the same brightness. As the moon come up it was still brighter than the moon.

"I've lived on the coast all my life and I've never seen anything like that. The sun was too low for it to be hitting the cloud formation. I've talked with other people about it and they don't know what it was either."

Very little information and no names are available on this. Many UFO witnesses don't want their names revealed. The witnesses were staying at the

Admiral Inn in Myrtle Beach, South Carolina, on May 13, 2011, when they witnessed an orange light that appeared over the ocean for a few seconds. It faded from sight and then two more orange lights appeared on either side of where the first one was initially sighted. The two lights faded out of sight. The lights were lower than the cloud cover. About ten minutes later, they suddenly reappeared farther north along the coast. One light was extremely bright and after a few seconds they were gone.

Other Reports from Along the Grand Strand

August 20, 1986, at 12:30 a.m.: Two friends were on the beach at Myrtle Beach. There were no hotels or high-rises in that area, so there were no lights to obstruct their view of the sky. The sky was clear and every star was visible. They were sitting on the beach looking over the ocean when one pointed to lights coming from over the ocean. As they got a little closer, they could make out six balls of light. The lights were blue, green, red, and orange and in a straight line. The first three balls were much larger than the last three. They were going from south to north, following the coastline. They were about two hundred yards from the shore and about one hundred feet above the water. They were not casting any reflection or glow on the water. There was no sound coming from the lights. The six lights went a short distance down the beach and then straight up and out of sight. About a minute later a red light came following the same path and went straight up and was gone. This lasted about four minutes.

July 1, 1995, at 3:15 a.m.: Two people were on the balcony of a hotel in Myrtle Beach when one observed five lights in a V formation. The lights were moving extremely fast and were very high in the sky. When they were directly in front of the hotel, they suddenly stopped and formed a circle. After a few seconds, they flew off in different directions at an incredible speed and out of sight. This lasted about fifteen seconds.

December 21, 1998, at about 2:10 a.m.: A motorist was traveling north on Highway 17 bypass in Myrtle Beach. While on a dark section of the road, the hood on the pickup started to glow a gold color. The color of the pickup was brown. The motorist observed a glowing green object heading north to northwest at medium speed. It continued in the same direction for about ten seconds and then all of a sudden it made a sharp angle left turn and disappeared over the horizon. When the motorist arrived home, he checked the weather channel to see how high the clouds were. The weather channel reported the clouds were at 10,000 feet. The light was below the clouds. The entire sighting lasted about thirty seconds.

September 10, 2007: With clear night skies over Myrtle Beach, a triangular object was seen hovering over the Atlantic Ocean just off the coast. A couple vacationing on the Grand Strand was staying on the twelfth floor of one of the high-rise resort hotels. The wife, being a night person, was sitting out on the balcony facing the ocean, enjoying the starlit sky, the surf, and the gentle ocean breeze. She had been sitting there for about thirty minutes when she spotted three lights, two white and one red, in the southeastern sky. At first they did not appear to be moving and were completely silent. She reached inside for her binoculars to get a better look. What she could see was a large, triangular-shaped object with more lights. There was a cluster of white lights and a small green light on the far end. She watched the object for about an hour and a half as it continued to sit motionless. The object appeared to be much larger than a passenger plane. It appeared to be about two hundred feet above the water. After about an hour and a half, it started to move slowly, and without any sound, toward the shore. It stopped and remained motionless for about fifteen minutes. She stepped inside and continued to watch it through the window. After about fifteen minutes, it slowly turned out toward the open ocean and floated away.

November 15, 2009, at 7:15 p.m.: A person with a background in aviation observed orange-colored orbs in the sky over the ocean at Myrtle Beach. He watched a single orange-colored orb suddenly appear over the ocean and move toward the coast. The light slowly moved over the land. At no time was there any sound from the light. The light hovered there for about three minutes or so, flew off to the south, and then straight up and out of sight.

July 21, 2010, at 9:30 p.m.: Two people observed three red-orange disc-shaped lights in the night sky over Myrtle Beach. The first light appeared, disappeared for about three seconds, and then reappeared. Soon another one appeared lower than the first one. The first two lights were joined by another one that appeared to be higher. These lights formed a triangle. The lights were the same shape, size, and color. They would fade in and out, one at a time. After several minutes of this, the lights completely disappeared. This lasted less than one minute.

November 11, 2010, at about 11:30 p.m.: Two people witnessed five red-brown lights over the ocean at Myrtle Beach. The lights were in a triangular formation, moving from west to east. The lights did not make a sound, and never changed from the triangular pattern. They were moving very fast and were soon out of sight. This lasted less than a minute.

November 18, 2010, at about 8 p.m.: Two people witnessed a yellowish-orange circle appear over the ocean. The circle was very bright compared to the stars. The light slowly faded out and then another one appeared to its left. This happened five times; as one would fade out, another one would appear. There was a considerable distance between the circles and no sound associated with them. The witnesses were about three miles from the ocean. This lasted about twelve seconds.

July 23, 2012: WPDE TV 15 news reported sightings of strange lights over Myrtle Beach. There were many witnesses to these lights, which were in the night sky for more than three hours. These lights did climbs and changed directions that seemed impossible for conventional aircraft. WPDE TV 15 interviewed several witnesses. MUFON reports indicate that others saw the same strange lights; these lights were reported to be coming from many directions and in different formations. The lights were flashing in different sequences. There were reports of orange spheres and white twinkling lights. The Federal Aviation Administration (FAA) stated that no pilots had reported anything unusual in the sky that night. Shaw Air Force Base reported that they were not conducting any training along the coast that night.

November 4, 2012, at 7 p.m.: One witness reported four or five bright orange lights in the Myrtle Beach sky. The lights were almost in a perfect circle and weren't moving very fast. After about a minute all of the lights vanished at the same time. The lights were between three hundred and five hundred feet in the air. Shortly after the lights vanished, an airplane was seen flying in the area where the lights had been. The lights lasted for about two minutes.

November 5, 2012, at 7:08 p.m.: Witnesses observed seven fireballs in a fleet formation. These fireballs were observed from two different locations within ten miles of each other. Three fireballs lit up in an orange-golden-amber glow and were moving slowly. Shortly after that three more lit up and followed the same direction. There were six fireballs visible now. They started to slowly fade out; they went out in the same order they lit up. As the last two faded out, another one lit up and followed the same pattern as the others. The lights lasted less than a minute.

(No date given): A former Navy officer was visiting Myrtle Beach, as he had been doing for the past twenty years. He was enjoying his favorite pastime, surf fishing. He was just a ways down from his hotel when he spotted an orange light appearing in the sky. It was a quarter moon, but it hadn't come up yet. The ocean was dark and there were no other lights on or above the ocean. The light got brighter and brighter as it got nearer. Seconds later a second light appeared and then a third one. The three lights formed a triangle, which remained for about fifteen to twenty seconds, before the first light began to fade. The other two lights began to slowly fade until there were no visible lights. This occurred three more times over the next fifteen minutes. It was the same sequence, but at different locations. The lights never got close enough to see an outline of the object or objects.

UFOS MAKE THEIR WAY AROUND SOUTH CAROLINA

Aiken

November 15, 1974, at 9 p.m.: Near Aiken, South Carolina, a very unusual craft was observed. The witness was in their backyard looking up at the stars when a parallelogram (rectangle) was spotted. It was approximately ten to fifteen miles up. It inverted (wrong-side up) itself and each time it would change color from red to green. The witness said it appeared to be two-dimensional because only the outline of the shape was visible. The inside seemed to be completely transparent. The object was traveling from east to west. It was visible for about thirty seconds and then the treeline blocked the view.

January 10, 2003: A slow, pulsating light flew over the first Aiken exit off Interstate 20. It crossed over the interstate traveling north to northwest. The object seemed to be long and kind of cigar-shaped due to the alignment of the pulsating lights. The witness turned on South Carolina Highway 19 and stopped to get a better look. The object was now stationary. A small aircraft was flying around, but not getting too close to the object. The object was in sight for about thirty minutes before slowly moving out of sight.

November 9, 2007, at about 1:30 a.m.: Two witnesses saw a cigar-shaped craft landing in a wooded area near Aiken. The witnesses reported that the object was a metallic cigar-shaped craft with no wings and no vapor trail; it was completely silent. When they first saw the object, it was about seventy-five yards away and hovering above a densely-wooded area. There were four square white lights evenly spaced on the top half. The entire craft had a soft metallic glow. The witnesses drove up the road and turned around for another look, but by then the craft had almost gone completely below the trees and out of sight.

August 1, 2008, at noon: The witness was fishing in a private lake near Aiken when he spotted a single black circle that suddenly appeared in front of a cloud. The black circle stayed stationary for about ten seconds before flying off at an extremely fast speed. It appeared to be a black circle with a circle around the edge outlined with a purplish blue light.

March 2008 (no day listed), at 8:23 p.m.: Two witnesses in Aiken observed three bright lights in a triangular shape near the International Space Station (ISS). At that time, the ISS was visible over the East Coast. The report said that the ISS moves at 17,000 miles per hour. The two witnesses were a forty-seven-year-old father and his sixteen-year-old son. They were outside watching the ISS when they noticed to the left of its path three bright lights much brighter than the stars. The lights would dim and then get brighter. When the ISS passed by, the three lights began to move and cross the path the space station had taken. They stayed in a triangular formation and picked up speed, flying off at an incredible rate.

October 30-November 1, 2010: The witness was on the way home when he observed a strange star that was pulsating different colors. He stopped on the side of the road to get a better look at the light. He stood so that the light pole was in direct line with the light so that he could see if it was moving or stationary. After staring at the light for three minutes, it had not moved. He headed home. When he arrived home, he got his camera and recorded eight minutes of video of the light and still no movement. When he watched it on his large screen TV, he could tell it was more than one light source.

The night of October 31st proved fruitless, and then on November 1st, he decided that he and his girlfriend would go outside again and see if there were any lights in the sky. This night would be the night of many unusual sightings. The first object appeared to be the same object that he observed several nights ago. This time the light was moving. It was descending toward the ground. At that time, three planes were in the air flying around the object. It slowly disappeared behind the trees. Just minutes later, two more of the same type of lights were observed, along with four more planes that were circling around the area with the lights. They watched the lights and planes for about fifteen minutes before going back inside. A few minutes later, they heard a very low plane come over their house. They went outside to see what was going on. This time they saw a light about fifty yards in front of the plane. The light was noiseless, but it had two dark yellow streaks of light behind it. Several minutes passed before they witnessed another object that made no noise and the lights on it were different than those on a plane. This object was directly overhead. It had a line of amber lights running from one end to the other. At the end was a bigger, much brighter light. They watched the lights until all of them disappeared.

Andrews

October 18, 2005: A man driving home from his girlfriend's house had just crossed Black River Bridge on Highway 41 three miles north of Andrews, South Carolina, when he spotted strange lights flashing in the night sky. The lights were orange and flashing in a rectangular pattern. The moon was out and brightly shining, giving the sky a deep purple color. The driver pulled off the road and exited the car in hopes of getting a better look. The lights were flashing and seemed to change patterns, as if signaling someone or something. As the object silently moved a little closer, the driver could make out that the lights were coming from a circular object. The driver reported that he felt like something was watching him. As the object moved away, the driver followed it in his car for about one-half mile before it disappeared into the night sky.

September 6, 2007, at 8:30 p.m.: Two people saw strange lights in the sky over Andrews, South Carolina. The four bright lights were hovering about twenty to thirty feet above the treetops and were in the shape of a kite. The lights were pointing towards the ground. The witnesses said they could see beams of light coming from the lights to the ground. The lights slowly started to dim and then completely disappeared. After the lights were gone, twelve twinkling lights appeared in the sky. The lights were moving in a northerly direction and kept moving until they were out of sight. Shortly after the lights vanished from sight, a small plane flew into the area where the lights started. The plane was quite low and flying very slow. The sound from the plane was the only sound that could be heard. There was no sound from the lights. The plane continued to fly in the area, circling back several times. When the plane turned and left, six twinkling lights appeared in the north and were coming back toward where the other lights were seen. All of a sudden all lights disappeared except one. It was a clear night with no air traffic except for the small plane. The lights were as bright as those on a football field, except they had a reddish tint. All the lights finally dimmed out and did not reappear.

Ballentine

November 10, 2012, at 9:10 p.m.: Two people witnessed a yellow-orange, egg-shaped UFO. The UFO was coming from the area of Lake Murray, moving over Ballentine. The first witness said he was outside getting something from his car when he saw the strange object. The object appeared to be yellow-orange as it came towards him. The witness called his wife outside to see the object, and together, they watched as it passed over them. There were no outside lights on the UFO, as it seemed to radiate light from inside. It wasn't a bright light…it just kind of lit the UFO up. As the UFO moved away, it appeared to be a yellow-white color. The UFO was much higher than the treetops, but much lower than the airplanes. It moved along smoothly in the night sky. There was no sound coming from the UFO. They watched the UFO until it moved out of sight behind some tall trees in a northeasterly direction.

Bishopville

December 31, 2011, at 10 p.m.: Two people watched strange lights in the direction of Florence, South Carolina. The lights had been appearing nightly for about three weeks in the same general area. On a clear night they were usually visible. The lights appeared to be strobe-like, alternating from blue to red to white and then to green. They don't flash in a pattern. The night of this report, the lights seemed to be closer than usual. They estimated the lights to be about twenty miles away.

May 30, 2012, at 7:30 p.m.: The witness was walking out to the corral and noticed what appeared to be white, blue, and red strobe lights in the sky. This was the second time this person has seen these lights. The lights began to move from the south towards the north very slowly. The lights stopped and hovered for a few minutes. When they began to move again, they left a bright white light behind. The white light lasted for about fifteen seconds and faded away, leaving a slight glow. The lights were still visible when the witness went back into his house. The witness watched the lights for about ten minutes.

Bluffton

January 29, 2009 at 6:25 p.m.: The witness was driving down the main highway in Bluffton, South Carolina, when she spotted a bright green, round-shaped object moving across the sky. It was traveling incredibly fast and shortly disappeared. There was no sound or visible trail left behind the object.

December 30, 2010: A witness reported seeing three lights moving in the sky over Bluffton. The lights were in the east, moving north. They were moving up and down; then one changed positions and then the other two lights changed positions, moving in an arc. The lights did not change color or intensity. There was no sound or smoke from the lights. The entire sighting lasted about three minutes.

October 1, 2011 (no time given): Three friends were leaving a friend's house and were walking home. One is the co-owner of an oil field service company, one was a psychologist, and the other was a fifth-grade teacher. All three were respected and creditable witnesses. They stopped to look at a light in the sky over Bluffton that one of them pointed out. The light was moving horizontally and then vertically at a very fast rate of speed. It would change direction to vertical without stopping. As the light got closer, they could make out the shape of a triangle. There was a light blue glow from the craft. They continued to watch the triangle craft performing impossible maneuvers. It would go straight up and down and then, without stopping, it would change directions and go from side to side very fast. They watched the aerial acrobatics for about fifteen minutes. There were several planes in the area, but the craft was much higher. The craft continued to move up and down and from side to side. They continued to watch the craft for about fifteen minutes until it moved out of sight. There was no sound from the craft.

October 1, 2011, at 11:41 p.m.: A 59-year-old woman witnessed an unusual event in the sky over Bluffton. The woman was looking at the stars when she noticed a UFO. As she turned to look at it, she saw a red and yellow flash of light going from the sky to the earth. There was an object in front and a trail of what appeared to be fire behind the object. This lasted about twenty seconds.

Charleston

October 4, 1998, at 9 p.m.: One witness reported seeing the sky light up over Charleston similar to what happens with heat lightning. All of a sudden a ball of fire came shooting across the sky. Sparks were going in all directions from the fireball, which appeared to be very low and much brighter than a shooting star. It lasted for about ten seconds and then vanished.

December 20, 1998, at 7:30 p.m.: A motorist reported seeing a green flaming ball of fire streaking across the sky over Charleston. The ball of fire was heading from north to south. The fireball was very big, very bright, and had a tail behind it. It lasted for about three seconds and then vanished from view.

March 13, 2000, at about 9 p.m.: Two people were visiting some college friends in Charleston. One evening the two friends decided to go down to the pier. They heard it was a popular destination around Charleston and they wanted to visit it. When they arrived, there were about one hundred people walking around the area enjoying the sights. They walked out on the pier to get a better look. As they neared the end of the pier, they saw a round- or oval-shaped dark object. They estimated the object to be about three hundred feet higher than the top of the bridge and larger than a football field, with maybe five hundred lights on it. The object was moving very slowly and there was no sound coming from it. The two friends looked around to see if anyone else had noticed the object, but it appeared that no one had. The other people were just going about their own business. The two friends were confused because no one else was seeing something this big — and that is where the memory of the two friends ends.

This sighting was reported on July 5, 2008 and the two witnesses still have no memory of anything after that. They cannot remember what happened to the object, or how they got back to their car or even their hotel room. They can't remember how much time is missing. They woke up the next morning with no memory until waking up. They continued their trip back to Washington, D.C.

June 20, 2001, at about 5:30 or 9:30 p.m. (two times are listed in the report): Five people witnessed a large orange-red sphere in the sky near Charleston. The object was in the northeastern sky. The stars were dwarfed by the size of the object. One of the witnesses had taken several classes in astronomy in college and knew this was not a naturally occurring phenomenon. Two of the witnesses watched the object through binoculars for about an hour. The object remained stationary and did not change colors until it started to fade away. When it started to fade away, it shimmered a shade of silver and then vanished. There was no sound from this object. The witnesses were ex-military, a media personality, a schoolteacher, and two nurses.

December 6, 2002, at 11:07 p.m.: A 34-year-old man witnessed a strange light in the night sky above Charleston. The sky began to lighten like you were turning on the daylight with a dimmer switch. All of a sudden a blue and yellow-orange fireball was seen coming from the west heading east. After about five seconds, it disappeared over the horizon.

November 14, 2003, at about 2:50 p.m.: Two people watching three planes spraying what looked like chemicals or smoke near Charleston saw a silver orb in the mist. One witness stopped at a park to get a better view of the planes. There was another car parked in the parking lot. She got out of the car to watch the planes also. They stood near the car watching the planes when they noticed a small flash of light at the junction of the trails where they made an X in the sky. The flash was only momentary. As they turned to watch one of the planes as it headed back over Charleston, they noticed a strange object in the sky. It was coming towards the park; it seemed to be gliding along and maintained a constant height and speed. It didn't appear to be too high. As the object got closer, they could make out that it was silver and appeared to be metallic and was perfectly round. There was no noise coming from the object. As the object got even closer, one witness reported he could see a violet haze around it. (The other witness didn't see the violet haze.) The object made a 180-degree turn and began to quickly ascend straight up and out of sight. The sky was clear with no clouds. This lasted for about five minutes.

April 29, 2005, at 9:10 p.m.: A lone witness spotted a blue boomerang-shaped haze. There was a light inside the center of the boomerang, which was traveling north to northeast. The witness reported that after watching the boomerang for several seconds a large sparkling (like a fireworks sparkler) something appeared for several seconds. After that there were two lights: the first light was sharp and bright, but the second light was hazy and moving slower than the first light. They continued to move in the same direction as the boomerang. After about five minutes they were out of sight.

Charleston Naval Base

October 10, 1975, at 5 p.m.: Just before dusk, the witness was standing in the parking lot of the commissary on the Charleston Naval Base waiting for his mother. The witness looked over to the northeast and spotted several flashing lights in the sky above the naval base; four or five flashing lights hovered in the same location for several minutes and then they flew off in different directions and out of sight.

Clinton

October 26, 1999: A resident witnessed an unusual triangle-shaped flying object. He was driving near Clinton when he first noticed the object. It appeared to have clouds around the outline and was moving toward the east at a brisk pace. It held the same speed until it reached some clouds and then slowed down and went behind the clouds. The witness could still see it a little through the clouds, but lost sight as he drove on. This lasted about four minutes.

Coward

November 18, 2008, at 7:30 p.m.: Several people, including a law enforcement officer, witnessed three lights blinking from red to white in the shape of a triangle pass directly overhead. After several seconds, the three lights spread out into a straight line. The lights were very close together and headed in a northeast direction. As they neared the horizon, they appeared to move up and down a little. The sighting lasted for about four minutes.

Darlington

October 5, 2009: While driving home late one night after work, a motorist was approaching the Darlington, South Carolina, city limits just minutes from his home. The driver noticed a red-orange light just above the treetops. At first the driver thought it was fireworks, but it didn't explode or spread out like fireworks normally do — it just remained stationary and continued to stay red-orange. After watching it a few seconds, two more red-orange lights appeared above the other light. The three lights remained motionless and soundless for a few seconds and then all three disappeared at once.

September 15, 2012, at about 10 p.m.: A circle of flashing lights were spotted over the city of Darlington. The two witnesses were outside doing some star-gazing when they spotted a star that started blinking different colors and appeared to be a circle of some sort. It was flashing multiple colors: red, blue, purple, pink, green, and white. The light would slowly fade out and then come back on and start flashing again. The light stayed in one place for about an hour and then faded out and was gone.

Georgetown

Late 1960s (no other date given), at about 8 p.m.: The sky over Georgetown, South Carolina, lit up with glowing colors. As darkness started to settle in, a massive explosion of glowing colors lit up the otherwise dark sky. Many Georgetown residents went outside to watch the dazzling colorful sky show, which lasted for about twenty minutes. I could not find any other information on this.

(No date given): A nine-year-old Georgetown resident was standing in the driveway at about 6:30 a.m. waiting for the school bus when he saw a triangle-shaped, silver craft. The weather conditions were overcast with a mild temperature. The silver craft was hovering a few feet above the treetops. There was no sound coming from the craft, which was shaped like a triangle with rounded edges and red and blue lights. The sighting lasted about three minutes.

September 26, 2011: Several Georgetown residents witnessed some strange lights in the sky while stopped at a stop sign. The first light was huge, bright, and white ball-shaped. As they continued on their way, still watching the first light, another one appeared. Seconds later a third one appeared. The first two lights faded out just as they had appeared. The original light shot off very quickly. The entire sighting lasted about three minutes.

Greenwood

April 15, 1991, at 6:15 p.m.: A UFO larger than a football field was spotted during daylight hours over Greenwood, South Carolina. The object was less than 150 feet away from the observers. There were no lights and the UFO moved silently through the air. The weather was clear and there were no planes in the area. Two brothers were outside at a friend's house when the UFO was first spotted. The first witness was looking up a slope at his friend when he spotted a large, oval-shaped disk over his friend's head. The oval-shaped disk appeared to be larger than a football field, taller than a three-story building, and almost transparent. As the witness ran toward the object, it flew out of sight very quickly.

February 7, 2009, at 2:04 p.m.: A UFO was observed following an airplane near Greenwood. The witness was walking back to the house after checking the mail when the witness looked up in response to the sound of an airplane flying overhead. The witness noticed in the distance behind the plane was a small shiny object moving in the same direction as the plane. The object began to slow down, to an almost complete stop, and then it began moving northeast. At the same time, a second object came into view behind it. Both objects sat there for several minutes before fading out of sight. The sighting lasted for eight minutes.

March 3, 2011 (no time given): Three people witnessed strange lights in the sky above Greenwood. The lights were in the direction of Matthews Mill. At first it looked like a bright light moving in their direction. They were standing outside of the Carlton apartments when they first observed the lights. As the lights got nearer, four lights became visible and a high-pitched sound could be heard. A second sound could be heard, which the witnesses said sounded like thunder rumbling in the distance, but there were no clouds in the sky. As it got closer to the witnesses, a large, black, oval shape was visible against the night sky and the noise got louder. As it continued to get closer, it made the witnesses' heads feel like when you get a pressure change in the mountains. It was moving slower than an airplane. No other information was given.

Two people driving home witnessed a slow-moving UFO for about two minutes near Greenwood. There was no sound at any time from the UFO.

Very bright lights were observed over the treetops. As they continued driving further down the road, they lost sight of the UFO behind the trees. They went about a quarter of a mile and made several turns trying to get another look at it. As they made their last turn, they could see the lights again. This time they were closer and the lights were much brighter. They could make out the shape until the UFO crossed the road and they saw it from an angle. It was a circle. They lost sight of it again as it passed behind some trees. The entire sighting lasted about two minutes.

August 27, 2012, at 11:55 p.m.: One person was in the yard going to the car when she witnessed lights in a triangle shape. The outside lights were white and the center light was red and blinking. The triangular-shaped object was flying from north to south. The craft was very low and made a slight rumbling noise. The triangle appeared to be between one hundred and five hundred feet high. About one minute later another triangular-shaped craft came into sight behind the first one, traveling in the same direction. The triangle-shaped craft were traveling about twenty to thirty miles an hour. This sighting lasted for about an hour.

Hemingway

November 7, 2005, at about 9 p.m.: Two reports were made of strange lights that appeared over Hemingway, South Carolina.

In the first report, there was only one witness. The witness noticed an orange light toward the west, and then several other lights started coming from the first light. They were all in a straight line. There was another light closer and just above the treetops. The lights started to slowly fade out in the same order that they appeared. A few seconds later, a streak of light shot across the sky. A few seconds after that, another streak of light shot across the sky from another direction.

In the second report, the lights lasted about four minutes. Witnesses said they first saw an orange light toward the west. After observing the light for a few seconds, they noticed that several other lights came from the first light. The lights were in a straight line. There was no sound, smoke, or vapor trail. Another light, which was farther away than the other lights, was moving just above the treetops. There were a total of four lights. The lights started disappearing in the order they first appeared. Within a few seconds, a fast streak of light shot across the sky twice, each time in a different direction.

Johnsonville

August 29, 2010: Security Officer Jack Smith was working the graveyard shift at a warehouse on Egg Farm Road, just outside of Johnsonville, South Carolina. Around 1:15 a.m., Smith checked in a truck. After checking with the truck driver, Smith returned to his patrol vehicle. Smith had just finished making notes on his patrol and turned the interior light of the vehicle off. Seconds after the interior light went off, the inside of the vehicle lit up like a vehicle had pulled right up behind the patrol vehicle. Smith got out of his vehicle to check on the other vehicle. There was no vehicle behind the patrol vehicle and the light was gone. After checking the loading dock and outside of the warehouse, Smith returned to his vehicle. There were no other vehicles on the property or the highway adjoining the property. It was a clear night, so there was no lightning.

Kiawah Island

June 6, 2009 (no time given): Two Kiawah Island residents witnessed a number of spheres over the Kiawah River. They kept appearing in groups of up to four spheres. At times there was only one sphere visible. At one point there was a sphere just outside their backyard about one hundred feet away. The neighborhood animals were going crazy. The spheres were visible for about an hour.

November 6, 2010, at 8:30 p.m.: Two Kiawah Island residents walked out on their deck and were startled by what they saw — eight to twelve very bright, orange objects over the ocean. The objects were in the southern sky and moving outward and up very fast. The night was clear with no air traffic. The lights started vanishing, as if they were evaporating. The sighting lasted for about ninety seconds.

June 6, 2012, at about 1 a.m.: The dogs in the Kiawah Island neighborhood started barking and going wild. One of the residents went out to see what was wrong with the dogs. He looked to the north and observed a round, red light moving toward the earth. It looked to be a few hundred feet above the ground. The witness went in to get his camera and when he returned, the light was gone.

Kingstree

February 27, 2007, at 8 p.m.: A 24-year-old military man and his wife (no information was given on her) saw strange lights in the night sky over Kingstree, South Carolina. The sighting lasted about two minutes. They saw a light that looked like a star, except it was bigger and kept going out for several seconds. The last time it went out and reappeared there was another light with it. They went out and reappeared with another light. Each time they went out and reappeared, they were in a different location. Finally, the lights went out again and did not reappear.

Lake City

December 16, 2001, at 9 p.m.: The witness observed a stationary light in the sky above Lake City, South Carolina. Shortly after the sighting, the light went out, but then came back on. There were several lights now in a zigzag pattern. All the lights went out again. Several minutes later, the main light reappeared and continued to remain stationary. It went out again, and when it came back on, it was across the sky. A small red light fell from it, and then both went out. This lasted for around ten minutes, and about ten minutes after that the area was saturated with airplanes.

December 17, 2001, at about 7:10 p.m.: A student reported seeing a big, round orange light in the sky over Lake City. Several seconds later, two or three more lights lit up near the first one. They were in a zigzag pattern. After several seconds, the lights connected and disappeared. Several minutes later, a number of airplanes were seen flying around in the area where the lights were.

Lake Murray

March 11, 2012, at 8:45 p.m.: A husband and wife were outside their Lake Murray home when they heard a rumbling sound over their house that lasted about two or three seconds. They looked up and saw an extremely large, fiery orange, round object hovering about five hundred feet above the house. The object was about as big as their house. The sky was clear, except for the stars and the fiery orange object, which was slowly moving in a northwestern direction. There was no trail from the object and no other noise. The object was visible for about three minutes.

Lancaster

September 30, 2009, at 11 p.m.: A Lancaster resident was walking his dog when he noticed how bright the moon was. When he looked away, he noticed three red, blue, and white lights flashing in the sky. At first they were in a straight line; then they moved into a triangular shape. Another light appeared in front of the others. At that time, a plane was flying into the area of the lights. Two of the lights flashed and were gone. There was another flash and the lights were back in a triangular formation. The plane continued to fly by the lights as if nothing was there. After the plane left the area, the lights lined up in a straight line again and faded out. The lights lasted about five minutes.

August 8, 2011, at 9 p.m.: Two Lancaster sky watchers were looking for the comet Elinin when they spotted what at first appeared to be a dim star. It started moving from the north toward the south — very fast. A second light appeared. Within five minutes, fifteen lights had appeared in various locations and were moving in different directions, some very slowly and some very fast. The lights were completely silent. One plane flew through the area during the light show. The sky was otherwise clear and void of any air traffic. One of the witnesses has been star-gazing for the past thirty years. The lights lasted about twenty minutes.

Laurens

February 5, 2001 at 10 p.m.: Two people witnessed a strange light over Laurens, South Carolina. They had gone outside to smoke a cigarette and were looking toward the east when they noticed a bright light in the night sky. The light was coming toward them from the east. It was moving very slowly. At that distance, it resembled an aircraft with its landing lights on. They spotted a plane coming toward the light, but it was higher up. As the plane neared the light, the light vanished. Seconds later, the light reappeared in the west. The light started slowly moving northwest. There appeared to be something there with several lights on it: a strobe and a green, and a red light. There were no sounds coming from the light. It slowly moved out of sight.

November 5, 2011, at about 2:11 a.m.: A V-shaped UFO with small red non-blinking lights inside of it was spotted over Laurens, South Carolina. The witness said he had spotted a similar object about eight months before flying low with no sound coming from it. It was flying just above the treetops. During the November 5th sighting, the UFO was moving faster, but the lights were not as bright. Like the first UFO sighting, this one disappeared into the distance in a very short period of time.

November 7, 2011, at 7 p.m.: Strange lights were spotted near Laurens, South Carolina. The lights were a burnt orange color and in a triangular formation. The lights were pulsating about every two seconds, but no noise was coming from them. They were moving south just above the treetops. After about two minutes, the lights moved out of sight.

Mauldin

January 24, 2007, at 8 p.m.: Several people witnessed a green fireball falling from the sky. The fireball was traveling very fast and appeared to get smaller as it fell. It appeared to hit the ground near Mauldin, South Carolina. This sighting lasted for about five seconds.

August 14, 2007: Two UFOs were sighted in the Mauldin, South Carolina, area. The first sighting was at 2:45 p.m. and lasted about one minute. The sky was clear and no airplanes were sighted in the area. The witness reported that he heard the dogs barking in the yard and went out to see what was the matter with them. When he got outside, he noticed a black, saucer-shaped object flying southwest toward the subdivision. It was coming in straight — and then made an abrupt turn toward the east. Within seconds, it had disappeared over the trees. About an hour and a half later, around 4:23 p.m., the dogs started barking again. The black saucer had reappeared. This time the saucer was traveling in a west to southwest direction. It headed toward Donaldson Airbase. There was no smoke, vapor trail, or sound coming from the craft.

Mount Carmel Campground

June 7, 2002, at 11:45 p.m.: Three people were on a camping trip at Mount Carmel Campground. The sky was clear. They were looking at the stars when all of a sudden a green rectangular light appeared. The light vanished and reappeared in another location. The light did that eight times, then made the shape of a circle. It did a ninety-degree turn and vanished. There was no sound from the light at any time. The sighting lasted about fifteen seconds.

Nesmith

November 19, 2011, at 11 p.m.: A family returning to their Nesmith home from a trip to Greenville, South Carolina, observed a strange looking star in the night sky over Nesmith. The light began to change colors and shift back and forth. The intensity of the light would change as it moved. What appeared to be a red laser streaked across the sky toward the light, which moved to avoid being struck by the laser. The light then returned to its original position and faded out. Was the military trying to shoot down an alien spacecraft with a laser? *Sounq goal ! (*

New Ellenton

No date given, about 6:30 p.m.: While driving near New Ellenton, South Carolina, two people witnessed a wingless, oblong-shaped craft flying very low. It had lights like an airplane, but didn't make any noise. The craft wasn't moving very fast…it was just coasting. The driver turned onto a side road to try to get a better look. He got out of the car and watched it change from a westerly direction to a northern direction. The craft didn't point that way — it just seemed to slide when it turned. They lost sight of it when it went behind the trees.

This next New Ellenton witness has several reports of the same type craft on different dates. The witness is an engineer and very familiar with conventional aircraft.

April 7, 2003, at 4:30 p.m.: The first report occurred when he noticed an unusually bright, white, glowing object in the direction of the Savannah River Nuclear Plant. He watched for several minutes as the light rose well above the trees. He could then make out an extremely large disc-shaped object, which was about a mile from the witness. At that point, the object had dimmed, but when it reached about 1,000 (estimated) feet, it became extremely bright white again. The craft hovered for a few seconds and then shot straight up. It traveled in an arc, heading south and out of sight. Several minutes later, it appeared again; this time, it was in the southern sky. It then traveled north at a high rate of speed and vanished over the horizon.

April 23, 2003, at 9:45 p.m.: The second sighting occurred when he first noticed what he thought was a very bright star just above the treetops. The light started moving higher up and across the sky. It was a circular-shaped object brightly illuminated in white to silver. The craft was traveling from south to north. The witness dashed inside his house to get his binoculars, and when he arrived back outside, it had reached the center of the sky. It moved in a zigzag motion, hovered for a few seconds, and then moved in a slight arc. When he looked at it through his binoculars, he could see that as it changed colors, it appeared to change shape. It would change from silver white to orange and then to blue and back to silver white. It appeared to be changing from a circular shape to an oval shape and then back to the circular shape. It took the object about three minutes to travel across his field of view. When it was just above the treetops, something separated from it and flew back in the direction it had come from.

North Charleston

February 13, 2003, at 12:15 a.m.: A husband and wife spotted a large V-shaped UFO in the sky over North Charleston, South Carolina. It appeared to be a solid object several hundred yards across. There was no noise associated with this UFO. When it passed under the stars, it did not cause them to blackout; rather, they seemed to shine right through it. It had four or five lights on each leading edge that were about as bright as the stars and about the same color. It had a very bright, flashing light following behind it. The UFO was moving in a northwestern direction out of sight.

March 24, 2005, at 11:40 p.m.: Near North Charleston, Luis (last name withheld) was waiting for his ride home when he decided to do a little star-gazing. He was hoping to see a satellite or a falling star when all of a sudden a round object appeared in the night sky. It was rapidly moving northwest. It was red on the sides, yellow from the middle towards the back, and the front edge was white. Even though it was very high, it appeared big enough for three passenger planes to fit in it. It was traveling in a straight line and much faster than conventional aircraft. Even at that speed, there was no sound heard from it. It did not create a sonic boom like planes do when they break the sound barrier. It continued moving in a straight line until it disappeared over the horizon.

July 4, 2010, at about 9:30 p.m.: A witness was in the hospital at Trident Medical Center in North Charleston, watching the display of fireworks out the window. The witness was looking towards Charleston Southern University across the street when they noticed a bright white light in a northwest direction just above the horizon. The light was about three times brighter than Venus and appeared to be stationary. The witness watched the light five to ten minutes before it just disappeared.

UFOs can even be spotted in daylight, as this next account shows.

October 10, 2010, at 1 p.m.: Two witnesses were outside watching airplanes crossing over North Charleston when a flashing light appeared. One witness reported seeing something like a light hit a mirror. The two witnesses focused their attention on that area. It was almost straight up. They noticed an object that looked like it was pulsating or flashing. After about a minute, it disappeared. They continued to watch the area where they had spotted the light, which soon appeared again. It pulsated or flashed and then disappeared again. Whenever it stopped pulsating or flashing, there would be nothing there — the sky was empty. After about another minute, it started again. After a few seconds, it disappeared again. This time, it did not reappear.

North Myrtle Beach

January 6, 2005, at about 1 p.m.: A Kentucky family vacationing in North Myrtle Beach spotted a round, gray object in the sky over the ocean while they were on the beach sunning. It was moving very fast at an altitude that allowed it to either go through or behind the clouds. They watched it for about forty seconds before it went behind a cloud. It did not reappear. There was no noise or smoke associated with the craft.

January 18, 2012, at 7:50 p.m.: The witness reported seeing three twinkling lights in the shape of a triangle moving across the sky at North Myrtle Beach. The lights formed a straight line and glowed a bright orange-red color, like a fireball. The lights glowed for about ten seconds and then disappeared. In less than a minute, they reappeared several miles farther out over the ocean. This time they were glowing orange. The lights lasted for several seconds and then disappeared. The lights made no noise and did not leave any kind of trail. The sighting lasted about four minutes.

August 7, 2012, at 9 p.m.: A family vacationing at North Myrtle Beach was outside when they noticed orange-red lights appearing in the sky over the ocean. They faded out. A few more appeared and faded out. They reappeared in another location. This sighting lasted about four minutes.

August 7, 2012, at 10:35 p.m.: A couple was sitting on their oceanfront condo balcony looking out over the ocean in a southeasterly direction when they noticed what looked like three reddish-yellow fireballs in the sky. They appeared to be several thousand feet apart and in a linear pattern. There was no movement from the lights, which continued to just hover there for about one minute, and then they just disappeared from sight.

October 2012: There have been a number of reports in the North Myrtle Beach area of orange-reddish lights or, as some describe them, fireballs, so two people decided to conduct their own field observation between 7:30 and 10:30 p.m. The date was October 5th. The two witnesses did not discuss their sighting with each other until the reports were made. One witness was well versed in astronomical, metrological, and aviation disciplines. The weather/visibility conditions were clear until 9:30 p.m. when scattered altocumulus clouds moved in at 10,000 feet. After about 10:15, it cleared up. The temperature was seventy-seven degrees; the barometric pressure was 29.95 in/hg. The wind was south at twelve knots. Some haze and ground lights restricted observation of stars to the fourth magnitude. Report from witness #1, the time of the sighting was at 8:35 p.m. The witness was sitting in a chair on the beach when a bright reddish-orange light was spotted in the sky. Witness #1 notified witness #2 of the sighting. Witness #2 had already observed the light, which traveled at the same altitude. After about fifteen seconds, it faded out to a pinpoint light. It traveled northeast and slowly faded out. The sighting lasted for about fifteen seconds. Witness #2 had a second sighting at 8:42 p.m. Witness #1 observed a bright reddish-orange light traveling very low to the horizon. The light began to rise higher into the sky. His light lasted about one minute. It was exhibiting similar flight characteristics of the first light. It was very bright at first and then faded to a white pinpoint light before disappearing.

The orange-reddish lights or fireballs are making regular appearances over the ocean at North Myrtle Beach, South Carolina This sighting was on October 22nd at 8:00 p.m. The witness was standing on the beach when he saw three orange-reddish lights appear over the ocean and last about eight seconds. The lights blinked out and reappeared in another location. One of the lights moved at a higher rate of speed and blinked out. The other two blinked out and were not seen again. On October 24th, the same witness and his girlfriend were on the beach when two orange-reddish lights appeared. They blinked out after a few seconds and reappeared farther away. After a few seconds, they blinked out and did not reappear. There was no sound from the lights either day.

Ocean Isle Beach

(No time given): The witness was facing north on Ocean Isle Beach when he heard a whirring sound. He looked east — toward the location of the sound — and saw a silver disc hovering above the ocean. It was about one hundred feet from the shoreline. The disc started slowly moving in a southeasterly direction, then flew out of sight.

Pamplico

February 19, 2003, at about 10 p.m.: A family was driving home from shopping when they saw a white light in the sky. Seconds later, another one appeared, followed by two more. After about a minute, all of the lights had disappeared. The sky was clear with no air traffic. Later, at home, the family was in their TV room when the daughter, who was looking out the window, started yelling. They went over to the window to see what she was so excited about, and they saw a large yellow light in the sky facing the window. The light started moving backwards and slowly disappeared. About five minutes later, they saw two more big yellow lights in the back field. They remained there for about a minute, then disappeared. The lights didn't move...they just disappeared. Seconds later, there were a lot of airplanes in the area.

Princeton

June 15, 1986, at 9 p.m.: A Princeton family witnessed a strangely shaped UFO. When they first observed it, the UFO was about seventy-five to one hundred feet high and moving at about five miles per hour. The unusually-shaped object was about seventy-five feet long, thirty feet wide, and ten feet high. The UFO was headed straight toward their house. It had very dim white lights; eight colored lights on the bottom appeared to be scanning the ground or searching for something. There was no sound from the UFO. The object was round in front and then tapered off to a narrow tube with a fin at the end. The color appeared to be a dull black. The witnesses reported that several months later lightning struck their house, destroying everything electrical.

Pumpkintown

Many UFO sightings are in small, rural communities or out-of-the-way places, such as deserted country roads and open fields out in the middle of nowhere. The following report is an example of one such sighting.

October 1 1972, at 11 p.m.: The sighting lasted more than thirty minutes and involved a boomerang-shaped craft with four bluish-white lights. The craft made a steady, low humming sound. The two witnesses were driving home on a deserted country road when they noticed a bright white light circling a large hill. They drove on without much interest because they thought it was a Ranger plane. All of a sudden it seemed to be following them. Sometimes the craft would be ahead of them and then behind them. They were driving between forty and fifty miles an hour, trying to keep the object in sight. The craft appeared to be about 1,000 feet high, though not very large. The FM radio in the car was being affected by an unusual amount of static. They had driven this road many times before and had never experienced any radio problems.

After several minutes, the craft veered off to the left toward a large empty field, came down to a few yards above the ground, and stopped. It was just hovering there. The two witnesses got out of the car and watched the craft for about two minutes until it started moving again. The object flew back into the air at about a forty-five degree angle. The witnesses said they could see the bluish-white lights on the leading edge of the craft. The craft was moving about twenty to twenty-five miles per hour. It was about 250 feet above the ground and about five hundred feet away. At this point, they could see the body of the craft against the night sky due to an almost full moon. There was no mistake — it was a boomerang-shaped craft. The craft continued to make a low, steady humming sound, which faded as the craft moved away and began to gain altitude. The craft suddenly stopped at about five hundred feet. The witnesses were able to stop the car under the craft, which remained motionless for about three or four minutes and then shot straight up and out of sight.

Reevesville

October 12, 2003, at 6:35 p.m.: The evening sun was sinking low just behind the trees. The witness was looking at the sunset when what appeared to be some kind of portal opened up. It was about fifteen to twenty feet above the ground and about fifteen to twenty feet wide. The witness reported that it was on her land. She tried to get her husband to come see, but he wasn't interested. The portal lasted for about fifteen minutes and then closed. She reported that a lot of strange things happen on her property, but always while she's alone.

Ridgeland

September 7, 2011 (no time given for this sighting): A resident reported a large unidentified craft hovering in a nearby field near the intersection of Route 278 and Wooden Horse Run. The craft was circled by an unknown number of white lights. After hovering for a few seconds, it sped off at a high rate of speed. The object was still visible in the distance until it flew out of sight.

Salem

December 27, 2005, at about 4 p.m.: Two people watched five lights in the sky for about an hour. The lights were in a triangular arrangement. It had one bright light in the middle and a smaller light above the bright light. Three smaller lights formed the triangular shape. The lights were just hovering in the same area, but from time to time they would kind of bounce a little. There appeared to be some kind of flares being shot inside the triangular area. The center light changed from white to red, to green, and then blue. The lights started moving in a diagonal direction and kind of bounced. The lights grew brighter and then dimmed out.

Scranton

January 29, 2011, at 2 a.m.: On a clear night, six red, orange, and blue lights were observed hovering in the sky. The lights were continuously flashing. No other information was given in the report.

Sniders Crossroads

February 12, 2002, at 1 a.m.: The witness was sitting in the living room listening to the radio when the front door swung open. The witness reported seeing strange lights just above the treetops. The witness went outside to investigate and watched the lights follow the treeline. The lights changed colors from red to green to blue and then to white as they moved. The lights were large and had a glow to them. There was no sound from the lights. The sighting lasted about a minute.

Socastee

August 13, 2006, at 10:30 a.m.: Seven people saw a strange object in the night sky while playing golf at the Witch course on Highway 544. They were on the course when they spotted a shining spherical object. There were some clouds, but the object was below them and in plain sight. The sunlight appeared to, at different times, reflect off the object. The object was slowly moving across the sky — there was no noise coming from it or trail behind it. It continued to move slowly along until it was out of sight.

Table Rock State Park

October 30, 2007, at 11 a.m.: A couple was checking out of a motel on South Carolina Highway 11, near Table Rock State Park, when the owner of the motel pointed out a silver, cigar-shaped object in the sky. The object was moving in a northwesterly direction. They could not determine the size, height, or speed of the object. There were no wings, tail, or lights visible on the object and there was no contrail or sound coming from it. The object appeared to be reflecting the sunlight. The sighting lasted only a few seconds before it went out of sight behind the trees.

Timmonsville

July 2, 2003: A 79-year-old Timmonsville man witnessed an oval-shaped UFO as he was pulling into his driveway. He observed a strange light about fifty to one hundred feet above the trees. The light was stationary with no movement at all. The oval-shaped UFO appeared to be about the size of a large car. There was no sound coming from it. The sighting lasted for about ten minutes. No other information was provided.

Electrical systems in cars will sometimes malfunction when in near proximity to a UFO, as this next story demonstrates.

August 16, 2005, at 9:15 p.m.: While traveling on a back road from Timmonsville to Florence, a motorist spotted a large, silver object flying low, approximately 1,000 feet high. Suddenly another one appeared. This one was kind of bluish and shot a light at the silver one — several small orange and blue lights came out. As the lights were flashing, the car radio began to get static on it and the engine started cutting out. After about three minutes, the UFOs disappeared, and the radio and engine went back to working normally.

October 19, 2008, at 7:30 p.m.: A man saw a cluster of flashing lights that appeared to be hovering in the sky over Timmonsville. At times some of the lights would slowly drift away from the others and then move back to their original position. Several times the lights disappeared completely, but then returned. The witness could not describe the size of the lights, nor could he hear any sound coming from them. This sighting lasted for about fifteen minutes.

Turbeville

July 19, 1975, at 10 p.m.: A thirteen-year-old boy saw a strange, twenty-foot by twenty-foot mint green light in his backyard. The light was about the height of a telephone pole off the ground. It was dark outside and the light was giving off a soft glow and lighting up part of the yard. The light was very bright and had a mist around the glow. The glow lasted for about thirty minutes.

The author, Sherman Carmichael, shares some of his own experiences in the next five accounts. These sightings occurred in Johnsonville, South Carolina.

March 22, 2012, at 8:36 p.m.: I walked outside the building where I work. The first thing I noticed was a group of nine lights in the southwest. (The human eye is attracted to the brightest color.) There were three triangles in a row, with three lights each. A light at each corner formed the triangles. The lights were much brighter than the stars. Nothing was visible except the lights. There was no outline of the triangle. The lights were bright gold and not blinking. The triangular lights were stationary; there was no smoke, sound, or trail of any kind. What appeared to be two military jets were fast-approaching the lights: one coming from the south and one coming from the west. As the planes neared the lights, they faded out — one triangle at a time — beginning with the first one. The two planes crossed over the area where the lights were and continued on their way. The lights were visible to me for less than one minute. The sky was clear with no clouds anywhere. There were a lot of planes flying that night and several nights before.

At 8:40 p.m., a single gold light — much bigger than the triangular lights — appeared. It was slowly falling and had smoke behind it. It went out all at once. It didn't fade out like the triangle lights. It appeared to be a flare dropped from one of the planes. It was farther toward the west than the triangular lights.

At 9:03 p.m., another single gold light appeared. It was much smaller, farther toward the west, and was slowly falling. It also had smoke behind it. It went out all at once — it didn't fade out like the others. It appeared to be another flare dropped from a plane. The planes continued to fly for about another hour.

Is the Air Force dropping flares in the areas of strange sightings to cover up extraterrestrial or terrestrial activity?

August 6, 2012, at 9:19 p.m.: I received a call from Jack Smith of Johnsonville, South Carolina. Smith was at work when he called. He said he had just seen a bright orange ball of light, completely round. "Fiery orange" is how he described the color. It was not a fireball, just the color of one. The sighting was at 9:05 p.m.

The light was stationary. There was no smoke or vapor trail, nor was it making any sound. Smith observed the light for about three to four seconds and then it just vanished. Smith did not know how long the light had been there before he saw it. The light was located toward the southwest. Approximately thirty seconds later what appeared to be a military jet approached the area where the light had been. The jet was traveling at a high rate of speed. The plane came from the north and went directly to the area where the light had been. Smith said what attracted his attention was the extreme brightness of the light.

Since I live close to the area where Smith works, I went outside immediately after the call and observed two more planes approaching from the west. By 9:31 p.m. there were seven planes circling the area where the light had been seen. At 9:32 p.m., one of the planes dropped three flares. Shortly after that, the planes left; some went toward the east and the others toward the south.

September 17, 2012, at 9:30 p.m.: I was standing in my front yard talking with a friend who is a law enforcement officer (name withheld) when I noticed some strange lights over toward the west. I could not distinguish the shape of it at first. It was traveling east at a very slow speed. The UAP (unidentified aerial phenomenon) came directly over my house — that was when I could tell it was triangular-shaped with six red and white blinking lights. There was no noise, smoke, or contrail from the UAP. There were a few scattered clouds, but the craft flew under them. It never left my view until it flew out of sight to the east.

I did locate a family of three who witnessed the UAP. They were returning home to Johnsonville from a trip to Florence. They were somewhere between Florence and Johnsonville. Names are withheld, and they wouldn't give their exact location.

March 11, 2013, at 8:50 p.m.: I was outside at my workplace when I looked toward the west and saw two large, four-point, star-shaped gold lights just sitting in the night sky. These lights were sharply defined and unusually bright. The light to my left was a little lower than the other light. At no time did either light move. I don't know how long they were there before I saw them. There was no air traffic in the area, and there was no smoke or trail behind the lights. I could not hear any sound coming from the lights. I observed the lights for about twenty seconds and then both went out at the same time. It was like somebody had flipped a switch and turned them off. There was a low cloud cover and the lights were below that, but still a good distance above the treetops. (I couldn't tell how high.) This is the third time I have seen strange lights in that area. You can read about my first sighting in my book *Forgotten Tales of South Carolina*.

April 3, 2013, at 9:03 p.m.: I was outside where I work when I noticed a very bright light in a northerly direction. It was traveling toward the east. Though it was much brighter than aircraft landing lights, the light was not moving as fast as a plane. When I first saw the light, there was no definable shape — just a bright light. As the light got closer, I could tell that there were three lights. I continued to watch them as they moved closer. The lights formed a triangular shape. I could not see any outline of a craft — just the lights — and then a fourth light appeared in the front. This light was so bright you could see it shining possibly miles ahead. The lights were very low — much lower than the planes that fly over the area. I did not hear any sound coming from the lights. When the lights were almost straight over my head, I tried to get a picture with my trusty cell phone camera. I had no idea what I was doing. I was moving the camera around, trying to find the lights, when I saw in the camera screen a line of six lights. The lights did not appear to be moving. I got a picture of the line of lights — they were amber, amber, blue, amber, blue, blue in that order. The line of lights faded out, while the triangular lights continued on and out of sight.

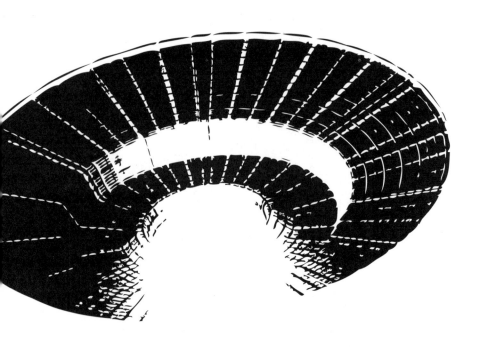

UFO SIGHTINGS ODDS & ENDS

A Visitor from Space

This story was sent to me from Susan Brown. I have contacted the newspapers and libraries around the area, but none of them had resources that I could get additional information on this story from.

It happened in 1960, but other than that I can't remember when. It was a Sunday evening after church when a friend asked several of us if we'd like to ride out to the area of Jack McInnis' pond and see something that his dad had told him about. His dad was a highway patrolman and the families were close friends and neighbors. He said his dad was on duty the night before and had come home and told them about a strange experience. He said there had been several calls in the county to law enforcement the night before about an unidentifiable bright light in the sky. I believe it was off a road between Clio and Tatum, South Carolina. A couple of patrolmen responded to the area and found a freshly-burned, charred crater near the pond.

When we arrived Sunday afternoon, there was yellow crime scene tape around it. It seems like I remember it being about one-third the size of a football field, with some fairly large chunks of some kind of metal-looking stuff scattered around. I don't recall this incident causing much of a stir around the area.

House Burns after UFO Visit

A South Carolina brother and sister reported to their parents about seeing the same UFO at different times and locations (the city is not named). The first sighting was the UFO hovering just above the trees near the daughter's school. A week later the same UFO was reported hovering above the house by the son. The cigar-shaped UFO was reported to be about twice the size of a single-story house.

About a week later, on February 9, 2008, at approximately 5 a.m., the daughter was awakened by a light outside her bedroom window. She went to the window and observed the same cigar-shaped UFO hovering outside their house. When she turned and looked back in her room, she noticed smoke coming up from the floor and woke the rest of the family. The family escaped without injury. The front of the house was completely engulfed in flames.

Did the UFO cause the fire or was it something else?

Antioch Community

From time to time, you get credible UFO witnesses that report missing time or waking up in a different place. This report has all three elements of a good UFO report. Both of these witnesses — a husband and wife — are professional people. The husband has a bachelor's degree and is a licensed pilot with fixed and rotor wing tickets. He also has an A and P mechanics license. He has worked in the aviation field since his second tour of Vietnam in 1969. He was a door gunner and later promoted to crew chief on Uh-1H Huey helicopters. His wife also has a bachelor's degree, and she has worked at the airport main terminal for the past twenty-five years. The Antioch Community is located near Gaffney, South Carolina.

On the night of June 7, 2008, at 11:00 p.m., they were returning home after visiting with friends. It was a warm night with a few scattered clouds.

The moon was very bright. They lived out in the country, so there was no traffic on the road. The wife was the first to spot the craft. She pointed it out to her husband. The craft was a dull black triangle-shaped craft with one purple light in the center of the bottom. There were no other lights on the craft. The craft was not making any noise. There appeared to be what could be considered windows in the craft. There was a dim light glowing from several locations around the craft. No life form was spotted.

The craft flew over the car and stopped at about the same time they pulled into their driveway. Since it was warm they had the windows down and the moon roof open. They remember the time being 11:20 p.m. when they pulled into the driveway. The next thing they remember was being in the car with the motor still running. The man, who was the original driver, was now sitting in the passenger seat. He is six feet five inches and his knees were killing him from being forced into the dash. His wife is five feet seven inches and she was in the driver's side. The seats they were in now were not adjusted to fit them. They closed the windows and the moon roof, turned off the car, and went into the house. The first thing they noticed was their atomic clock read 2:24 a.m. Three hours and four minutes were missing. They didn't remember anything after pulling into their driveway. The next morning, the man woke up with a headache. His wife, meanwhile, felt so bad that she stayed in bed most of the day.

Furman University

This UFO story was sent to me by the owner of Shelor and Son Publishing Company, Derik Shelor. During his sophomore or junior year at Furman University in the early 1990s, he witnessed something he can't explain. Shelor and some friends were outside the student center near the ATM. Shelor looked up and noticed something overhead. It was a craft of some sort. All he could see was the silhouette of it. It was shaped somewhat like a helicopter. It was thicker in the front and slender towards the back. There were no rotors visible and no sound from the craft. It was just silently moving overhead. Shelor estimated the craft to be about one hundred feet high. There was no air blowing down from the craft, and no smoke or contrail. It had two lights, one in front and one at the back. The front light was red and the back light was white. There was no static electricity in the air and no smell of fumes or exhaust. The craft was visible for about fifteen seconds. Shelor did not point this out to any of his friends.

More UFO Sightings

Author's note: No locations given for this next group of sightings.

December 28, 1999: Two motorists traveling to North Carolina on Interstate 85 spotted two very bright orange-red fireballs in the eastern sky. They appeared to be over the ocean. The fireballs were traveling from the surface of the earth up into the night sky and then all of a sudden they were gone. The fireballs were about the size of a full moon. There was no sound associated with these fireballs.

January 24, 2007, at 8 p.m.: Many residents of South Carolina reported seeing blue and green lights streaking through the sky towards the ground. The Sheriff's office in Greenville, Pickens, and Spartanburg counties reported receiving dozens of calls concerning these strange lights. The reports varied as to the exact color and number of lights being seen.

December 27, 2007, at 8 p.m.: Bright lights were seen in the sky above South Carolina. The light show lasted for about fifteen minutes. The three witnesses were traveling on Interstate 20 when they observed the strange lights. The lights appeared to be circles in the sky, playing or dancing with each other. The lights formed a straight line, then went together, then separated, and then went together to form a circle. The lights disappeared, reappeared, and remained ahead of the witnesses' car. They exited off the Interstate for a short break. When they returned to Interstate 20, a single bright light appeared and remained there for about five minutes.

September 13, 2010, at 10:45 p.m.: A South Carolina woman witnessed a cylinder-shaped UFO moving down vertically in the sky. It had three bright lights (no color was given for the lights). The background around the object was blurry and distorted as if the UFO was putting out some sort of an energy field that distorted the surrounding area. The object was about one hundred feet away and right above a church. A passenger in a vehicle, as they drove along, the woman continued to watch the UFO out the back window. It soon faded out of sight behind the trees. The woman convinced the driver to turn around and return to the location of the sighting, but when they arrived, there was nothing there.

As with most UFO sightings, information is sketchy at best. This next one has almost no information.

August 19, 2011, at 6 p.m.: A large, gray, disc-shaped craft was observed traveling east beside an airplane, which was also heading east. Both were very high, though a height could not be determined. It could not have been a reflection because there were no clouds between the sun and the airplane. The observer looked away for the briefest of moments and then looked back — the UFO was gone. The plane continued flying east.

January 12, 2012, at 1:23 a.m.: A former United States Air Force Crash Rescue Team member was responding to a structure fire when he noticed a very large, cigar-shaped craft moving very slowly. The craft was just above the treetops and three hundred to four hundred feet away from the witness. The object made no sound at all. The sky was clear with an almost full moon. The witness also observed the object through night vision monocles. The craft had no wings; the body was very long, about twice the length of an aircraft. The red blinking light was on the front and the two white lights were on the back. It took about one minute for the craft to cross the witness's yard. It slowly moved over a very large open field. As he pulled out of his yard and looked to his left, the craft was gone.

An ex-Air Force crewman with 2,750 hours in an Air Force aircraft witnessed a round metallic object in the daylight sky. The witness was parked in the parking lot at St. Francis Hospital when he spotted the unknown object. The sky was clear with a small cloud deck at about 2,000 feet. The witness saw a flash of light like the sun reflecting off a shiny, metal surface. This reflection came from straight overhead — that's when he noticed a round metallic object sitting stationary just below the cloud deck. All of a sudden it accelerated from a hovering position straight up into the cloud at a tremendous speed. The object did not come into view again.

January 26, 2012: A witness reported ten spheres with flashing white lights moving erratically in the sky. These strange lights were accompanied by a low-flying, triangular-shaped craft. The witness received a call from a friend about twenty miles away that had just seen these objects. The witness went outside and saw ten spheres with flashing white lights moving in strange patterns. They were moving in all directions. The sky was clear that night. The witness's wife joined him outside. She saw a triangular-shaped object with three lights about a quarter mile above the ground. It was moving very slowly and made no noise. They watched the object move west for about five minutes and then it turned and came in their direction. This lasted for about fifteen minutes. The craft went out of sight over the ocean. About twenty minutes after losing sight, they saw three helicopters in the area, including a large one that appeared to be using a search light.

CONCLUSION
Just a Thought

From ancient cave dwellers that left their stories recorded in drawings and paintings on cave walls to modern-day presidents, astronauts, and high-ranking military personnel, UFOs are well documented.

Throughout recorded history, UFOs have been visiting earth and have left their mark: the Great Pyramids of Egypt, the Mayan ruins of Central America and Mexico, Stonehenge, Easter Island, and the Nazca Lines, just to mention a few. The list could go on and on.

In modern times, sightings of UFOs have increased dramatically. Not just in America, but worldwide. You can't deny that something is invading our air space and the government seems powerless against it. Who or what controls our air space now? Do we have control of our own air space? The presence of an advanced race of intelligent beings from somewhere other than earth is no longer something that can be denied or argued against.

Scientists and the government can't tolerate the truth about UFOs and alien beings coming to earth. If this is happening, then our uninvited guests would know more than the scientists and our world leaders and they don't like to think that anyone or anything knows more than they do.

There is undeniable evidence that humans are being abducted by aliens, and these abductions are happening at an alarming rate. Does the government know about this? If so, are they okay with it? Of course they know about it, but is there anything they can do about it? There is no way to prepare against an alien abduction…no one knows when or where it will occur. If they want you, they will get you. Some people have reported being abducted several times; other abductees never report it. Some may not know they have been abducted while others are afraid of what people will think. Some abductees can only remember what appeared to be a dream and some have been returned with implants. Are these implants tracking devices or instruments to monitor the functions of the body?

The government won't admit that there is such a thing as a UFO or that there is life on other planets. Some refer to this as ETVs (extraterrestrial vehicles). They simply say that UFOs don't exist, or it's a misidentification. The government has a way of covering up what they don't want us to know about. If it takes destroying a person's reputation or career to cover it up, then that's okay with them. They don't mind using threats to intimidate those who have witnessed UFO sightings. The government just can't admit that UFOs are real, nor can they admit that there's a power here that they have no control over. The government is helpless when it comes to UFOs. The UFOs come into our air space at will, stay as long as they want to, and then leave.

Another thought. Is the government in contact with the occupants of the UFOs and allowing them to go about their business unrestricted?

There have been gods in every culture and time from the beginning. These gods performed amazing feats and miracles that can't be duplicated today with all our modern technology. Were these gods alien visitors from a distant galaxy here to help a primitive society? Are they still helping our primitive society?

Some religious groups believe UFOs are satanic and that these alien visitors are messengers from Hell, sent to pick a certain few to spread Satan's message, or that they are dark overlords in the service of Satan, sent forth to corrupt mankind.

As we stand outside at night, gazing at the stars, they shine in the sky in all their splendor. It's hard to believe that someone or something is looking back at us. Or is it? With the innumerable number of stars that we can see, it is hard to believe that something that could create all of that would create only humans. But then humans have an ego problem. We want to believe that we're the only living beings ever created — that would make us special; a superior race, when, in reality, we just might not be special or superior. We might not be as important in the grand scheme of things as we would like to think.

Why do we feel so superior to think that the maker would only create us? Take a look at the heavens — maybe we're just a tiny, insignificant speck that those superior beings are just watching to see how long it will take us to destroy ourselves. Will those beings that are paying us regular visits stop us from destroying ourselves or continue to monitor us and let us carry out our plan of self destruction?

UFOs are a daily occurrence. Someone somewhere is witnessing a UFO right now. They seem to come in all shapes and sizes from the giant triangle- or cigar-shaped craft to the tiny spheres that we see in the night sky. Of course, we don't know that any of those tiny little lights are UFOs. Many of those can be explained as misidentification or airplanes. I watch a lot of UFO videos and none of those distant, tiny, twinkling lights convince me that they're UFOs. Most of those turn out to be airplanes. It's those witnesses who witness a craft of some sort that have a good UFO case and there are lots of those.

Space flight for us began only a few short years ago, as NASA was founded in 1958. The first human in space was the Russian Yuri Gagarin on April 12, 1961; the first American was Alan B. Shepard Jr. on May 5, 1961. If history is not lying to us — and I don't believe it is — then we have been visited by space travelers since the beginning of time. The evidence of aliens visiting us is recorded on every continent in the world. Many believe that the modern technology of today was brought here by visitors from somewhere else. Many believe that alien visitors have been helping us since the beginning of mankind.

Some possible explanations for UFO sightings are military aircraft, civilian aircraft, and the planet Venus, which appears to move. This is an optical illusion. Fog, haze, and clouds can distort the image you think you see. A camera lens can distort a point of light and make it resemble a saucer-shaped light. With a sighting, the visual impression of the distance from the object or the speed of the object is very unreliable. It's all based on assumed size and speed. Most UFOs are seen against a clear sky or a dark night sky with no reference points to set a maximum distance, size, or speed. However, there are thousands of UFO reports yearly that cannot be explained.

There are those who don't believe that UFOs are visitors from distant planets. In the early nineteenth century, John Cleves Symmes (1779-1829) sought funding for an expedition to the center of the earth. His plan was to take an expedition through one of the polar holes. Syymmes was convinced that an advanced civilization existed there. Even today hollow-earthers believe that UFOs come from the center of the earth. The people in the UFOs are descendents of Atlantis and Lemuria.

There are those who have a more scientific approach to the UFO theory — black holes. If black holes do exist in our universe, where do they lead? Maybe to another universe? In theory, black holes suck in everything around them and there's no escape from it. Some scientists believe there are white holes that are the exact opposite of a black hole. Matter is expelled, rather than swallowed up. What if an advanced civilization had discovered a way to control flight through a black hole? They could leave their universe through a black hole and enter our universe through a white hole. When the visitors returned to their universe, they would enter a black hole in our universe and exit the white hole in their universe. Of course, this is just in the theoretical stage for us.

Another possible connection between two points in the space time of the same universe is through an Einstein-Rosen bridge, also known as a wormhole. Perhaps this advanced civilization is using the black hole to travel through time. Maybe these beings that are visiting us on a regular basis are time travelers. Maybe we're being visited by beings from the future. After all, in many UFO sightings, the UFO is there one minute and gone the next…as if it just disappeared.

DEDICATION

To Beverly Carmichael, Ric Carmichael, James Ebert, Derik Shelor, Will Finch, Milton Finch, Susan Brown, Lynne Ebert, Mark Watkins, Jack Smith, and Cindy James

INDEX